# THE GOOD SENSE OF JESUS

# THE GOOD SENSE OF JESUS

## A COMMENTARY ON THE BEATITUDES

FR. IVÁN PERTINÉ

TAN Books
Charlotte, North Carolina

Cover design by Caroline K. Green

Library of Congress Control Number: 2018963001

ISBN: 978-1-5051-1334-1

Published in the United States by
TAN Books
PO Box 410487
Charlotte, NC 28241
www.TANBooks.com

Printed and bound in the United States of America

Praise for *The Good Sense of Jesus*! Experience it and know Christ Jesus like never before!

The book *The Good Sense of Jesus* is very illuminating. I would highlight its distinctively Christian approach, the clear and decided proposal for the "life in Christ," the presentation of the Beatitudes with its clarifying elucidations, the "Decalogue to achieve peace," and the description of the faith as a response to a Presence.

—Daniel Cardinal Sturla, Archbishop of Montevideo, Uruguay

This is not a book to read quickly, nor one to read and set down. You won't be able to. It is a book for praying, for dialoging with the Lord, and also for dialoging with the author from one's own lived experience.

At the end of each talk or chapter, Father Iván leads you to enter your own interior world and offers opportune questions for assimilating the content and seeing where you stand spiritually.

I am certain that, once you've finished the book, you will experience with Father Pertiné that "the teaching of Christ is the most sensible, the most fitting for the human heart and the best response to our deepest desires . . ."

—Bishop Santiago Olivera,
Ordinary for the Military Services in Argentina
From the prologue to the original Spanish edition

These pages will show that Fr. Iván has clearly been "seized" by Christ. He is completely taken up with him and driven to share his love, to make him known. There is no greater happiness for human beings, no greater beatitude than Christ himself. "Blessed are those who know Christ!" this book wants to shout, wants to insist, wants to show the way.

—Abbot Jeremy Driscoll, O.S.B.
Abbot of Mount Angel Abbey
Chancellor, Mount Angel Seminary
From the prologue to the English edition

I dedicate this book to all the members
of the Saint John Society.

# CONTENTS

# FOREWORD TO THE SPANISH EDITION

IN his introduction to this book, the author, Father Iván Pertiné, makes it clear that this work is the fruit of a retreat he preached to the priests of the Saint John Society, of which he is the general director.

That is why I don't need to speak about that in my prologue, but I do want to share my own experience of receiving this book and receiving at the same time the request to share with all of you what the reading has generated in me. And even though Fr. Iván explains that it was thought about, prayed about, and preached to the priests of the Saint John Society, the universality of what is Christian and Catholic can do great good for all members of the Church.

The Saint John Society is a Society of Apostolic Life born in the bosom of the Diocese of Cruz del Eje, the diocese for which I have had the joy of being pastor for the past eight years. This holy land is preparing to receive the first Argentine priest saint, of the diocesan clergy of Córdoba, our beloved Saint José Gabriel del Rosario (Saint Cura Brochero).

It is here, in this diocese, where the society's "missionaries took their first steps," approved by then-Bishop Omar Félix Colomé, and for this reason the link with the society has been one of esteem and closeness, from the time of its birth until now.

I thank Father Iván for asking me for this favor. As often happens, the favor was really for me. I began reading and finished reading, very much praying this book from the first pages.

Reading and praying about the Beatitudes and the Sermon on the Mount in this year of mercy has been a very special grace.

This is not a book to read quickly, nor one to read and set down. You won't be able to. It is a book for praying, for dialoging with the Lord, and also for dialoging with the author from one's own lived experience.

At the end of each talk or chapter, Father Iván leads you to enter your own interior world and offers opportune questions for assimilating the content and seeing where you stand spiritually.

I am certain that, once you've finished the book, you will experience with Father Pertiné that "the teaching of Christ is the most sensible, the most fitting for the human heart and the best response to our deepest desires."

+SANTIAGO OLIVERA,
Bishop of the Diocese of Cruz del Eje, Córdoba, Argentina

# FOREWORD TO THE ENGLISH EDITION

I am happy to introduce English readers to this book by Fr. Iván Pertiné, a book translated from the Spanish. It shares extensive meditations on the Beatitudes that Fr. Iván first prepared for members of the Society of Apostolic life of which he is the director, the Saint John Society. The Saint John Society was founded in Argentina, but it has subsequently expanded to Uruguay, the United States, and Italy.

I have known Fr. Iván and members of his society for some fifteen years now through their association with us at Mount Angel Abbey and Seminary. I came to know him as he has watched over the formation of students of the society who studied with us. I observed him with admiration as he and other members of the society worked in pastoral settings in the Archdiocese of Portland. During these years, my regard for him and the ideals of the society only grew. The members have a deep heart for the New Evangelization, and they very effectively call people to the Gospel, either for a first time or in renewal.

This is why I am happy that this book is available now to English-speaking readers. Although the conferences collected here are directed to priests of the Saint John Society, the reflections can be enriching for any reader, and they are a beautiful window into the spirit of this vigorous and energetic society. Access to the spirit of this society is why this book is important. By following Fr. Iván's conferences, the reader can enter into the details of how the society's members are formed: how they think, how they pray, what they learn to care about, and how they increase their zeal. Preaching the Gospel not only with words but with the authenticity of one's own life is a very serious undertaking. And here we see Fr. Iván challenging the brothers of his society to the continual conversion that is required of disciples of Christ and servants of the Gospel. Now, by means of this book, this serious effort by the members of the society can become an example and stimulus for others.

The meditation on each beatitude is extensive. The words of Jesus are meditated on in their own right, but then they are explored with many styles of further reflection by Fr. Iván. For example, he may share his own or others' struggles with what Jesus is saying. He works through these and shows a way forward. He brings rich texts from past and present to bear on the different beatitudes—in one moment Chrysostom or Ambrose or Augustine and in another Pope Francis or Pope John Paul or Newman or Aquinas. This wide-ranging drawing on the richness of others is typical of the Saint John Society. These are the ingredients of what I noted there is to emulate in them: how they are formed, how they think, how they pray, what they learn to care about, and how they increase their zeal. All this is shared now beyond the society and with the reader of this book.

It is not difficult to detect in what one reads here that the original setting for this material was live conferences from the director of the Saint John Society to his brother members. This suggests a way to use the book. It probably will not be too helpful to just settle in and read it straight through. Rather, I would suggest using it as workbook. It would be best to read slowly, not too much at once, and then plan some time for prayer and thought afterwards. This is the way that Fr. Iván is conducting the retreat, aware that his brothers in the society are framing his conferences with their own prayer and reflection. I'm suggesting that a reader do the same. Every beatitude is concluded with proposed exercises. I'm sure that many readers would profit from following through on these as well.

These pages will show that Fr. Iván has clearly been "seized" by Christ. He is completely taken up with him and driven to share his love, to make him known. There is no greater happiness for human beings, no greater beatitude than Christ himself. "Blessed are those who know Christ!" this book wants to shout, wants to insist, wants to show the way.

ABBOT JEREMY DRISCOLL, OSB
Abbot of Mount Angel Abbey
Chancellor, Mount Angel Seminary

# INTRODUCTION

THIS book was born from a retreat that I preached for the priests of the Saint John Society. The proposed topics were the Beatitudes and the Sermon on the Mount. Well aware of the challenge of presenting these chapters of the Gospel of Matthew, I dedicated a year to praying with these texts and to reading different studies and commentaries about them.

The Sermon on the Mount is one of the passages of the Word with the most commentaries, from the Fathers of the Church until today. It is in some way beyond our grasp; it won't allow itself to be domesticated or reduced to an idea in a manual. Rather, it has life and dynamism, and it asks us to question ourselves and awakens in us a deep desire to live as it suggests: totally before God, free from unnecessary attachments, and completely given over to the mission to which we have been called.

I preached these reflections as a retreat to priests, and later—with a few adaptations—to different groups of lay people in Argentina, in Uruguay, and in the United States. Finally, I preached it to the missionaries of the Saint John Society, who, while studying philosophy, are preparing to become priests at the service of the New Evangelization.

In each of these retreats, my comprehension of the text grew richer from the experience of so many people who, each in their own place and context, strive to be faithful to the teachings of Jesus and to live this Word with evangelical radicalism. For this reason, these pages are in a way written a little by all of them and are born from the back and forth both with God in prayer and with my brothers as I preached to them and listened to their life experiences. These reflections were first a simple written text that was later preached and finally transcribed. This explains the oral style of these pages. These are talks that were given live; therefore, the transcriptions are agile and informal in their expression so that reading them is like conversing with friends. I decided it was best to conserve this oral rhythm because it expresses the communitarian dynamism in which these reflections began to take form, and because it is an invitation to the reader to "sit for a retreat" and participate in it as another retreatant.

Naturally, since this book is the version of the retreat preached to the missionaries, the readers will encounter allusions to the Saint John Society, to its constitutions, to consecrated life, to the challenge of the New Evangelization, and to some circumstances of the recent history of the birth of this Society of Apostolic Life.

This is written as a retreat for men who want to consecrate themselves to Christ in the Saint John Society. But I believe much of what is shared here can be profitably read by all and adapted to the personal circumstances of each reader, because those who are called to follow Christ in his public life through the streets of the Galilees of today aren't made of different material but rather are "taken from among men"[1] for his service. And because Christ is a man

---

[1]    Heb 5:1.

among men, he can "deal patiently with the ignorant and erring, for he himself is beset by weakness."[2] That which is useful for some is useful for all, and vice versa, if it is read with faith and in prayer.

This leads me to make a suggestion: at the end of each chapter, there is an exercise, a proposal for prayer with the Beatitudes and with the Sermon on the Mount. I make a heartfelt invitation that you complete these exercises so as to configure yourself to Christ and experience in your life "the glorious freedom of the children of God."[3]

At the end of the Sermon on the Mount, Jesus compares the man who listens to his teaching and puts it into practice to a wise man who knew how to build solidly: "Everyone who listens to these words of mine and acts on them will be like a wise man who built his house on rock. The rain fell, the floods came, and the winds blew and buffeted the house. But it did not collapse; it had been set solidly on rock."[4] And he contrasts the wise man with the fool, who listened but did not practice, and so built on the sand, and the house collapsed in the storm. The comparison is suggestive. Listening and putting what we hear into practice is the most sensible option, which allows us to build and to orient our lives according to the criteria of the Gospel.

Often, it is said that living the Gospel is very difficult. In reality, I believe that it is the easiest thing, in the long run. It is difficult to live without God, seeking blindly and alone. It is easier to listen to the Gospel, to belong to a Christian community, to walk with others, and to benefit from the

---

[2]     Heb 5:2.

[3]     Rom 8:21.

[4]     Mt 7:24–25.

wisdom of the Church. It is difficult to be alone, and it is difficult, because of its mid- and long-range consequences, to live in submission to one's own passions and the pressure of the criteria of this world. In contrast, life is easier and simpler when I am capable of entrusting myself to the Word, struggling against myself, and so advancing in the interior freedom that allows me to love more deeply. It is true that doing so implies a free choice. The Word of Jesus does not appeal to what is most superficial or instinctive but rather to the deepest level, the most personal and free, where we make our decisions. But it is also true that the one who has taken this step begins to experience that the teaching of Christ is the wisest course, the most fitting for the human heart, and the one that best responds to our deepest desires and to our common sense. *His teaching is wise, and it makes us wise.* So everyone who practices the Sermon on the Mount, with the grace of God, enters into the paths of Christian wisdom and recovers the good sense which comes from having the fundamental existential coordinates; that is, we are children of the Father, we have been and are loved by God, we are pilgrims headed to heaven, we have to sow while there is time and also cultivate a fraternal life, of this life we will only bring with us what we have given, and so on.

"May the God of our Lord Jesus Christ, the Father of glory, give you a spirit of wisdom and revelation resulting in knowledge of him. May the eyes of your hearts be enlightened, that you many know what is the hope that belongs to his call, what are the riches of glory in his inheritance among the holy ones, and what is the surpassing greatness of his power for us who believe, in accord with the exercise of his great might."[5]

---

5    Eph 1:17–19.

# THE HUMANITY OF JESUS

I invite you to begin with great courage. As we know, reading a spiritual book implies entering into it with strength, since its fruits and its lights depend in great part on the way we approach what the book wants to transmit to us. The need for a strong beginning is a constant in the spiritual life. That is why we insist on how positive it is to leap out of bed when you first wake up and to make a morning offering at the beginning of the day.

Beginning with great courage, with generosity, and with faith is very important. I think that the desire to go to meet the Lord with our lanterns lit, with courage and generosity, is already an act of faith. Praying is already an act of faith. I go to the chapel in the morning with the belief that the Lord has a word for me, a grace to give me, that he is going to touch my soul. Sometimes I will feel it more, sometimes less, but every day I go with faith.

Faith is a gift of God that must be put into practice; it mustn't be taken for granted. It is also a human response to the gift from God. That is why I encourage you to enter into these pages with great courage.

## Jesus, the Glorious Man

The prologue of John's Gospel says, "And the Word became flesh and made his dwelling among us, and we saw his glory."[1] Scholars say that when John is writing about the glory that he saw, he is not referring so much to the miracles or to the resurrection of Jesus (although he doesn't exclude them) as he is to Jesus's way of being a man. *Jesus was a glorious man; his humanity reflected the glory, the beauty, the light of God . . . humanly.*

For John, the death of Jesus was glorious: the serenity, the love, the self-giving, the way in which he triumphed over hatred and sin. In reality, it was glorious for Christ as well. John saw this glory and highlighted it.

The Apostle John was one of the first to follow Jesus. When he was called, John saw, stayed with Jesus that day, and proclaimed that he had encountered the Messiah.[2] The human gestures of Jesus—his conversation, his way of treating others—were an eloquent sign of his identity. And in his first letter, John the Evangelist wrote, "What we have heard, what we have seen with our eyes, what we have looked upon and touched with our hands concerns the Word of Life—for the life was made visible; we have seen it and testify to it."[3] He was a witness of the glorious humanity of Jesus.

So now we might ask ourselves: what does it mean for me to "contemplate the humanity of Jesus"?

It means entering into the texts of the Gospel that reveal this portrait of Jesus Christ and using our imagination, intelligence, feelings. *It means letting Jesus reveal himself to me, letting him touch my ascetic effort to pray and, with the grace of the Spirit, show himself to me. That I might see*

---

[1]    Jn 1:14.
[2]    See Jn 1:35.
[3]    1 Jn 1:1.

*his humanity, contemplate it, and so see my own. See his humanity and see my own humanity in order to conform mine to his.*

That is why, together with John, we ask him: *Lord, let me contemplate your humanity. Let me enter into your glorious humanity.*

### Jesus Is Present and Comes to Serve Me

For Matthew, Jesus is "he who is with us." He presents him in this way with great power: he is Emmanuel. He who at the beginning of the Gospel is announced,[4] who in the middle of the Gospel promises his presence saying, "Where two or three are gathered together in my name, there am I in the midst of them,"[5] and who at the end assures us: "I am with you always, until the end of the age."[6] Jesus is the God who is here.

As we begin these reflections, let's make an act of faith in the presence of Jesus in our midst. He is not only present in the Eucharist; that is a given. Jesus is engaged with us in this reading; he is involved, and he is interested in it. He is interested in each one of us; he is here in this house, here in this place. Jesus is here: here listening, waiting. He is really present.

The hymn of Philippians that we pray during Vespers every Saturday describes the ascent and descent of Jesus: "Though he was in the form of God, Jesus did not deem equality with God something to be grasped. Rather, he

---

4   See Mt 1:23.
5   Mt 18:20.
6   Mt 28:20.

emptied himself, taking the form of a slave, coming in human likeness; and found human in appearance."[7]

Jesus didn't only fulfill this in his incarnation and live it in his public life, but rather continues to repeat it and relive it. *He comes even to us today, in the form of a slave.* And in these days of retreat, *Jesus comes to serve us. He is among us in these days to wash our feet as he did for the apostles at the Last Supper, to listen to us in prayer, to give us advice as a friend, to speak to us, to give us light.*

I invite you to make an act of faith and to address him with joy, saying, "How humble you are, my God, to be with me in these days!"

Let us ask to see his glory as we make this retreat. *This teaching of the Sermon on the Mount is glorious, unsurpassed, unsurpassable. The Beatitudes are glorious, and he is glorious, he who lived them to the fullest.*

## Salvation Comes From Jesus

Allow me to read you an excerpt from an article that I like a lot. It is so beautiful! It says:

> Because only God creates, only the fiat of God is creator: "Let there be light." The fiat of Mary, who conceived the only son of God, was a prayer. It wasn't a heroic act on her part, it wasn't her own capacity; it was a prayer: "Here I am, let it be done, let it happen."
>
> "Let it be done" is a request, and that is how she conceived virginally and virginally gave birth. How important is the *virginis in partu* of Mary! How important it is to accept the certainty of faith that she gave birth virginally! Because salvation doesn't come from suffering, but salvation comes

---

[7]    Phil 2:7.

from grace. It doesn't come from our sufferings; salvation comes because we are loved. It doesn't come from the suffering of man: salvation comes through the joy of God, from the fullness of the joy of God. Salvation comes because we are loved. That Mary gave birth without suffering, that she gave birth without violence, that she gave birth virginally, that is to say, in wonder . . . it is a sign that salvation comes because we are loved.

The certainty of faith about the virginal birth is summed up by Pius XII in *Mistici Corporis* with this expression: "in a marvelous birth." While each one of us has come into the world through birth with pain, that birth was a birth of astonishment, without pain, without violence, because salvation comes from grace. Salvation isn't born of sin, it's not born of the desert; it blossoms in the desert and makes the desert blossom, but it comes because we are loved. The fact that we are loved is born of the happiness of God. We are loved because of the superabundance of happiness that is the Trinity; we are loved through the superabundance of correspondence that is the eternal love of the Father and of the Son that we call the Holy Spirit; we are loved by Grace.

Mary's childbearing, *the marvelous birth that Mary gave is a physical sign, a carnal sign that salvation does not come from us, that salvation does not come from suffering, that salvation does not come from pain, that salvation does not come from the cry of man. Salvation comes by the Grace of God. Infinite happiness through the superabundance of happiness, by the superabundance of Grace.*[8]

That is to say, salvation comes through God's initiative. He comes to save us, not because we have struggled much nor because we have overcome or have conquered, but

---

[8]    Giacomo Tantardini, "La Humanidad de Cristo es nuestra felicidad," Catedral de Fidenza, published December 20, 2006, http://www. 30giorni.it/articoli_supplemento_id_22145_l2.htm. Translation is mine.

rather salvation comes to us through the superabundance of love because we have been loved first. A sign of that, this author writes, is the virginal birth of Mary: a serene delivery that couldn't have come about from the humanity of Mary alone. It was a visible sign from on high, as was her virginal conception.

### God Calls You!

God saves us by reaching out to us where we are, and this is happening again right now, not because we will it, but rather because the Lord loves us and, in his providence, invites us so that he can give us his grace and his love. He calls us.

I remember when we began to give retreats, years ago. The retreats at that time were similar in style to the Cursillo retreats. There we often heard this question: "Do you think you have come to this retreat because someone invited you? No! You have come because God called you!" These words seemed to me to be a bit grandiose, a bit theatrical. "Is it true?" I asked myself. But now I realize that it *is* true and that those words pointed to a profound truth of faith: he called us.

Salvation comes from above, from God's initiative in life. You go to a spiritual retreat, or you read this book, because he called you to be here: he loved you and he sought you.

That is why I invite you to say your *fiat*: "Let it be done to me." In this first meditation, say it like the Virgin Mary, with great willingness. *Let it be done to me, Lord, whatever you want to make of my life: what you want to break, what you want to purify, what you want me to offer. I don't want to make a cosmetic change, but rather to work in the depths. If you want me to take big steps, I will take big steps; if you want them to be little steps, they will be, . . . but I come with a willing spirit.*

And after pronouncing this *fiat*, I propose that you ask for a grace for your spiritual life. A grace, a gift from God that you are needing: the gift of deeper prayer, the gift of a more profound chastity, the gift of confirmation in your vocation, the gift of greater peace, the gift of apostolic zeal, the gift of greater austerity or poverty of life, the gift of a simpler and more humane friendship with others, the gift of touching hearts with your own life and preaching. Whatever you are in need of, ask for it. Later, surrender your prayer there, at the feet of Jesus, and . . . let yourself be led by him!

Finally, I invite you also to look back at this year, since your last retreat, from the perspective of grace. The questions that I suggest for this are the following: "What is it that God wanted to do in me? What is it that he could do in me?" We can also think about anything that maybe he could not work in us because he didn't encounter the necessary collaboration.

# LIFE IN CHRIST

## Jesus Is the New Moses

IN the first part of the Sermon on the Mount, the Gospel says, "When he saw the crowds, he went up the mountain, and after he had sat down, his disciples came to him. He began to teach them, saying . . ."[1] And the Beatitudes begin.

We know that in the Sermon on the Mount Jesus presents himself as a new Moses, as *the* new Moses, in fact. The one who comes to give the new law, the new covenant, and the new grace. That is why he goes up the mountain, like Moses did in order to receive the tablets of the law. Jesus goes up the mountain to give the new law, to teach the Christian lifestyle.

Jesus went up the mountain and sat down in the attitude of a teacher, just as the important rabbis taught, and his disciples came to him, going up to where he was. "He began to teach them, saying . . ."

This is, in some way, the solemn initiation of his teaching: sitting down, settling in, having his disciples come to him and sit on the mountain. And then Jesus, the Master, the one who teaches, begins to teach them, saying all that he has to say.

---

[1]    Mt 5:1–2.

## Being a Disciple

We're going to delve a bit deeper into this: what does it mean to be a disciple of Jesus? It means they draw near to listen to his word. This is a teaching for disciples: it presupposes an interest in listening to Christ and an effort in climbing the mountain. It's not a teaching that Jesus gives in the middle of the streets, in the plazas, or in the synagogues, where there are Jews who listen to him simply because they are there (although he also taught in those places, giving missionary sermons for the lost sheep of the house of Israel).

But this is a preaching for his disciples, for those who have an interest in leaving their homes, climbing the mountain, sitting down, and listening to what he has to say. This is not a mere ethical or simple moral teaching, but rather a specification of what discipleship means: a person who is connected to Jesus as the master and teacher and who has proclaimed himself a disciple of Christ.

That is why for us the first step in the spiritual life is to recognize Jesus as master: *He is the one who teaches me; I am the one who learns. He is the one who questions me; I am the one who lets myself be questioned. I am not the one who challenges his teaching; rather, his teaching challenges me. It is not the teaching of Christ that has to be adapted to my life, but rather it is my life that has to be adapted to the teaching of Christ. I am the one who needs to be formed, reshaped, touched, and transformed. I have to learn, because I don't know how to live this way; I haven't yet learned.* His teaching is not in me yet, at least it is not in me fully.

Therefore, in this first meditation, I would like you to

proclaim yourself a "disciple" of Christ, to go to prayer and say to him: *Lord, I want to climb the mountain during these days. I want to sit down and listen to your word, and I proclaim myself your disciple. You are my Master, the one who has to teach me, and I am the one who needs to learn.* Ask for the openness and humility of the disciples, who don't always understand every point. A disciple is one who is close to the master. He is close to him and learns from what the master says, from what he doesn't say, from what he does, and from what he doesn't do. The disciple becomes permeated by the master.

Being Christ's disciple implies the decision to constantly stand before his Word, viewing my own life in the light of his teaching. And in order to do that, there are certain texts that are the gold-standard, if you can talk about the Gospels like this. These texts have been anointed by generations of Christians who have prayed with them and molded their lives around them. These texts include: the parable of the sower and the call for us to be fertile land;[2] the parable of the prodigal son, in which the mercy of the Father is presented to us in a moving way;[3] the parable of the talents, with its urgency to multiply the gifts received;[4] and the parable of the final judgment, in which we are called to practice the works of mercy.[5] The incalculable influence of this last text can be attributed to so many hospitals, asylums, soup

---

[2]   See Mt 13:3–9, 18–23.
[3]   See Lk 15: 11–32.
[4]   See Mt 25:14–30.
[5]   See Mt 25: 31–46.

kitchens, care-homes . . . so many congregations dedicated to the service of the poorest.[6]

Among these golden passages, reigning over them, are these three chapters of Matthew, chapters 5 to 7: the Sermon on the Mount.

Let's take a brief moment, then, and proclaim ourselves disciples of Jesus.

A disciple experiences a call from Jesus. Jesus called each disciple personally, not only his apostles. He seeks them and calls them to himself. Jesus says in the Gospel of John, "No one can come to me unless the Father who sent me draws him."[7] That is to say, being a disciple implies already having been touched by the grace of God, having been found by him, as St. Paul says when he exclaims, "I continue my pursuit in hope that I may possess it, since I have indeed been taken possession of by Christ Jesus."[8] I have been found by him, taken possession of by him; that is why I am his disciple. This is the "New Situation" found in Christ Jesus, a new life that begins when we live with him daily.

To be saved does not only mean to be forgiven, or even only to go to heaven after our death. It includes both but has a richer and more dynamic meaning. It is about our transformation from the broken creatures that we are, as sons and daughters of Adam and Eve, into sons and daughters of the Father, in Christ, by the Holy Spirit. It is about moving from an old situation to a new and better one. It is about communion and love with the triune God.

---

6    Mother Teresa of Calcutta constantly taught her sisters to count the five fingers of her hand, saying: 1) you 2) did 3) it 4) to 5) me.

7    Jn 6:44.

8    Phil 3:12.

Therefore, we cannot live the Beatitudes and the Sermon on the Mount unless it is in the grace of God, in the grace of Christ, grafted onto him. *We cannot be disciples of Jesus just by an effort of exterior adaptation, but rather there has to be an interior transformation which, in a living discipleship, is produced, is given.*

But *Jesus is more than a role model or an interior force of transformation.* The master, like a sculptor, carves the life of the disciple with a two-sided chisel. On the one hand, we have the chisel of the Word that shapes us from the outside, because when we go to the Gospels, we are confronted with the life and teachings of Jesus. On the other hand, the chisel of the Holy Spirit forms us from within through the grace of God.

### Participation in the Life of Christ

I would like us to take some time to consider the mystery of *the grace of God, that inserts us into Christ* and permits us to be his disciples. We know that grace is a participation in the life of Christ, but I would like us to go deeper: what, concretely, does it mean to participate in the life of Jesus?

How can I participate in the actions, events, and sentiments of another person's life, the person of the Son? These actions, events, and feelings occurred so long ago: the day-to-day events of his infancy, his youth, his public life, his itinerant preaching, his acts of love for the poor, his righteous anger, his self-giving, his forgiveness of sins, his death, his resurrection. How can I participate in all these things that have already happened? And what, concretely, does this mean for me?

We are our own persons, separate from others and separate from Christ. We are individual beings, and our individuality connects us, but also separates us. We are individuals who live in a specific time and place, are immersed in a particular culture, and have our own history.

How can I participate in the life of another person who lived two thousand years ago? How can I love him? How can I follow him? What's more, how can I participate in the life of another person without ceasing to be authentically myself?

This isn't a speculative or theoretical question; rather, it is very practical because the answer is at the heart of our life. It's a question that's important for all Christians, but even more so for those of us who are priests and missionaries.

Let's imagine, for example, a dentist. How can a dentist participate in the life of Jesus who was an itinerant preacher in Palestine? What does the one life have to do with the other, beyond the essential: imitating Christ's charity and love for neighbor? *How can this man not only follow Christ's teaching but participate in the life of Christ even as he rides the bus and works in his clinic?*

Those of us who are priests and missionaries, who seek to live the public life of Jesus, how can we participate in his life? *We are called to be a prolongation of the humanity of Christ.* Saint Elizabeth of the Trinity described it as a "supplementary humanity,"[9] *a new incarnation of Christ in the world.*

---

[9]   "I sense my powerlessness and beg you to clothe me with yourself. Identify my soul with all the movements of your soul, submerge me, overwhelm me, substitute yourself for me, so that my life may become a reflection of your life. . . . O Consuming Fire, Spirit of Love,

*We can participate in the life of Jesus because we participate in the grace of Christ.* And the grace of Christ is the participation in the humanity of Jesus in his divine nature.

## The Human Nature of Jesus

Jesus—as a man with human intelligence, human will, human feelings, human desires, and a human body—participated in (i.e., took part in, was penetrated by, as if bathed in, as if illuminated by) the divinity of the Eternal Son of the Father, who is the one that assumed his human nature and sustained it.

He participated in a unique nearness to God in his human nature, participated in the hypostatic union. And therefore, there was something like a constant ebb and flow between the grace of God that bathed his humanity, and his humanity that responded to that grace of union with generosity, with self-giving, with fidelity. It was an ebb and flow founded in the permanent dialogue between his human intelligence and his divine Sonship, between his human feelings and his divine Person. It was a perfect correlation.

The human nature of Jesus was fully permeated by the Holy Spirit. Time after time, from the womb of the Virgin Mary and throughout the moments of his life that we know from the Gospels, he received various anointings of the Holy Spirit. And each time he responded to the presence of God in his life. He was God, obviously, so when I speak about his response to the presence of God, I am referring

---

overshadow me so that the Word may be, as it were, incarnate again in my soul. May I be for him a new humanity in which he can renew all his mystery." St. Elizabeth of the Trinity – "Prayer to the Trinity."

to his human nature responding freely to God. The union of his human nature in the Person of the Son—the hypostatic union—permeated and inundated his humanity completely, not nullifying it, but rather realizing it. This is unique to him. For example, how did Christ pray as both man and God? His prayer was unique to him. But what we do know about him is that there was a free, human response to the presence and grace of God in his nature.

With time, it grew in Christ because he always responded with fidelity; it became perfected. That is why the Gospel of Luke says that "Jesus advanced in wisdom and age and favor before God and man."[10] The capacity of his human nature increased in the measure that he grew.

With each affirmative response, the human capacity of Jesus to welcome the grace of God increased. At the same time, his response—as well as his actions, feelings, and attitudes—was not only a response to grace but also permeated his own identity. This also happens to us. Each thing that we decide, each thing that we do, in some way permeates our own identity. As we live, we configure our identity.

Jesus, humanly, developed his identity as a man throughout his whole life, and all of his choices remain in him, in the same way that our childhood, youth, and all the choices we've made remain in each of us. *We are partly our history, and we are also partly our future, our calling.*

---

[10]    Lk 2:52.

## The Spirit Connects Us With the
## Human Nature of Jesus

To participate in the grace of Christ is to participate in his humanity, because that same grace, *that same light that permeated the humanity of Jesus, is given to us through the action of the Holy Spirit.*

It's as if you were to take a sponge, that is the human nature of Jesus, and soak it in perfumed water, that is the grace of God, and then take the sponge and squeeze it out over another person—something like that. The perfumed water is the grace of the Spirit that soaked into the nature of Jesus, (the sponge,) and later is placed on your head. You are soaked with that same water which came to soak the human nature of Jesus, and it enters into you.

Now in your own life you have the spirit of another; you are really and mysteriously connected with another person, with another human nature, with another human intelligence, with another human will, with another's human feelings, with another life. *You are mysteriously connected with the life of Jesus through the action of the Spirit, who wants to breathe that other life into your life.*

*That other life isn't a theoretical life but rather a real life that has already been lived. It is the life of Jesus. It's not a life from a manual, but a concrete life. It's not that the Holy Spirit wants to make you better, more patient . . . No. He wants to make you more like Christ, and that is why he wants to make you better and more patient.*

*The Holy Spirit wants to make us more like Christ* as he unites us to him. And that is why we participate in his birth, his infancy, his youth, in his love for the poor, in his preaching, in his cross, in his resurrection: all of that is in us through the grace of the Holy Spirit.

Through Baptism, we are "buried," says the Word of God;[11] we are plunged into Jesus and transformed into new men.

Listen to the letter to the Romans: "For we know that our old self was crucified with him, so that our sinful body might be done away with, that we might no longer be in slavery to sin. For a dead person has been absolved from sin. If, then, we have died with Christ, we believe that we shall also live with him."[12]

And there are many other texts that speak of this: "You are not in the flesh; on the contrary, you are in the spirit, if only the Spirit of God dwells in you. Whoever does not have the Spirit of Christ does not belong to him," St. Paul says.[13]

*It's that simple: you cannot be a disciple of Christ, you cannot be of Christ, if you do not have the Spirit of Christ.* "But if Christ is in you, although the body is dead because of sin, the spirit is alive because of righteousness. If the spirit of the one who raised Jesus from the dead dwells in you, the one who raised Christ from the dead will give life to your mortal bodies also, through his Spirit that dwells in you."[14]

---

[11]   See Rom 6:4–6.
[12]   Rom 6:6–8.
[13]   Rom 8:9.
[14]   Rom 8:10–11.

## Christ Integrates Me Into Himself

My love for Christ and his love for me is made possible through the grace of the Spirit. This grace communicates this new life to me through the sacraments, especially when I receive Communion. Receiving Communion is the most tangible physical expression of this: *I eat the Body of Christ, and Christ integrates me into himself.* But it is also true of all the sacraments through the actual graces they communicate. *The grace that we receive is a kind of synthesis of the life of Christ that can be unfurled in us; it is there as if condensed, but later it spreads out in me.* It's as if I could take someone's life and condense it, condense it, condense it . . . Then I give that concentrate to another person, who puts it in water, and it begins to grow again in the person who receives it.

Something like this happens with Jesus's life. All the mysteries of his life are communicated to us, and they gradually unleash their strength. The mysteries of the life of Christ are linked to the liturgical seasons, and his grace is spread out in consonance with the rhythms of the Church, which is why we have Easter and Christmas.

This real bond of love between us and Christ begins to reconfigure us, to make us like Christ. It's a little like what happens with people who live together and care about each other. Often you can see this in yourself: "I'm a bit like Fr. Pablo in this" or "I'm more like Fr. Willy when I do that," or "I sound like Fr. Christian when I say this!" Each one is already part of you.

Life together, shared objectives, friendship . . . they begin to give us something in common. When you're with those you're closest to, you know where they're coming from when they say and do things because you've shared a common experience, part of them is in you. They are part of your own identity. This happens to us in the Saint John Society: we recognize attitudes that stem from the SSJ, but which now are fully ours. We don't experience this as a form of alienation but rather as a growth in our deepest identity because we have been called to this society; it is second nature to us. The same thing happens among members of a family: they have a commonality among them which, if the relationships are healthy, they are proud of.

Well, something like this happens to us in Christ as priests. That is why *our spirituality is the life in Christ, living in him, growing in him until I reach my full maturity, the stature to which I have been called.* St. Paul says that Christ so organized us "to equip the holy ones for ministry, for building up the body of Christ, until we all attain to the unity of faith and knowledge of the Son of God, to mature manhood, to the full stature of Christ."[15] This maturity in Christ, to which we have been called, is personal to each one of us.

This phenomenon also happens to all Christians, including the dentist, who has also been called to maturity in Christ. He, too, if he is a Christian, participates in the human nature of Jesus.

How can the life of the dentist synthesize with the life of Jesus, which is so different from his own? Yet that is his vocation; that is the synthesis that only he can produce. *Each one of us reflects the life of Christ in a unique way,* just

---

[15]    Eph 4:12.

as the crystals of a chandelier do. Each tiny mirror reflects the light and refracts it in a different way. That is why *no one is replaceable. We are unique and unrepeatable.* Each one has his own specific vocation. The dentist's vocation is to merge his life with that of Jesus, despite the vast differences in the two. The dentist will live his life reflecting the life of Christ as a Christian dentist. St. Alberto Hurtado said, "Jesus desires to have actions in his mystical body that he didn't have in his mortal body: he wants to be a soldier, an aviator, a mother, a university student, to grow old, to become sick with cancer, to be a mountain climber, to teach a child . . . how? In us and through us, who live his life working under his impulse."[16]

For those of us who are priests, our vocation is even more direct: we are called to reflect Christ the preacher, Christ itinerant, Christ missionary, Christ celibate, Christ poor. The likeness is clearer and the connection stronger because the life of Christ really was this way: Jesus really was a preacher and a missionary.

I remember when I turned thirty-four, I felt a certain sadness. "Jesus was never thirty-four," I thought. "How will the life of Jesus be reflected in me since he was never thirty-four? Will the grace of God reach me here or will I be left without it? Maybe now that I'm thirty-four I will fall into emptiness . . ."

But no. The grace of God continued to unfurl in my life. *Jesus wants to do things through his mystical body that he*

---

16    Alberto Hurtado, "Un disparo a la eternidad," in *Retiros Espirituales Predicados por el Padre Alberto Hurtado, SJ,* (Santiago de Chile:Ediciones Universidad Católica de Chile, 2002), 131.

*never experienced in his mortal body.* Jesus never was forty-four, as I am now. But he wants to be forty-four years old in me so that I can do even greater things in him. When Jesus said, "You will do even greater things,"[17] he means that we will do things that he didn't do: "You will go to all the world,"[18] for example, to preach the Gospel. "You will take an airplane," "You will use the internet," etc.

That is why spirituality is *living in him*, being united to him through the grace of the Spirit, that he may live in me today. Spirituality is the rationality of man penetrated by the Holy Spirit, which transforms me so that I can be in relationship with God, with the world, with myself and with others . . . in Christ.

### Spiritual Life Grafts Us Into the Heart of Christ

In philosophy we learn that the human being is spiritual by nature (lowercase), that he is spiritual because he has intelligence and will. Are we in agreement?

Because he is spiritual, everything around him is a "world," instead of simply "surroundings"[19]: he is open to the totality of things, the whole of reality, because he asks himself about the totality. Intelligence is the capacity to encompass the whole of reality, and through the will, he is capable of loving each thing. Therefore, the human being will not, like the animal, be limited by his vital interests, but rather beyond his vital interests, he will relate with

---

[17]   Jn 14:12.

[18]   Mt 28:19.

[19]   See Josef Pieper, *Leisure, the Basis of Culture* (San Francisco:Ignatius Press, 2009), 95.

the whole of reality, at least potentially. That is why he is spiritual.

That is why *spiritual life is the spiritual condition of the man grafted on to Christ. It is this relationship with the whole of reality "from and in" the heart of Christ that creates a new situation in our lives.* This new situation in Christ makes us children of the Father, brothers to all people; it saves us and gives us a mission in the world. It transforms all of our relationships by grafting them on to Christ Jesus.

We are called to grow in this graft, to constantly grow and deepen our spiritual life. We are invited to participate and collaborate in this dynamic of grace.

*Holiness is dynamic, it grows. I am not the same as when I was first ordained a priest.* I have grown in humanity through the impact of the Holy Spirit. Regrettably, along with the growth there has also been regression. But, after adding and subtracting, I sense that I have grown overall. And I believe that this is a natural part of Christian life.

That is why the spirituality that we live and foster is very simple. It gets at the essence of being Christian: to live in Christ, to be fully connected to him.

We are connected if we live in the grace of God, but our collaboration is not forced. Connecting with Christ in me is an exercise of the will: *Lord, you are in me, I am in you. This is what my old self would want to do, but this is what you want me to do as a new man.* In this way, we begin to learn to connect with that interior fountain "that springs up to eternal life."[20]

It is as if in our heart there were two doors, like the

---

[20]    Jn 4:14.

floodgates of a canal, the doors that open and close in order
to direct the flow of the water: in each situation, one door
opens to my old self and the other opens to Christ—or
sometimes, each is open halfway.

For example, let's say I need to study. I either start to
study as my old self or I begin to study from Christ within
me. Maybe exteriorly someone who observes me can't see
any difference, or maybe he can, but interiorly, there is a
difference. I either study in Christ or I study alone; I speak
with someone in Christ or I speak to him alone; and so on.

Let's suppose that I am taking the train home at night
from the center of Buenos Aires, and the environment of
the train is a little sordid. Well, I can take the trip alone or
I can take it *in* Christ. I can say: "Lord, you want to travel
here with me, you want to be a living presence in me and
in this place today. How can I travel with you and connect
with you, you who are in me? Teach me how to love these
people in some way, even though right now I can't do anything for them. Let *your humanity permeate my humanity in this moment.*" As I pray, I open the door to Christ,
and in that moment, living water flows from the canal and
begins to irrigate the field of my intelligence, my will, and
my feelings.

And that is how I am able to be transformed in Christ.
Still, we don't always open the floodgate; we don't always
allow that water to irrigate all of our humanity. We have
to open the gate time and time again. Our connection to
Christ is always there, but since we are always changing
and find ourselves in different situations, it is very important that we allow Christ to irrigate us again. These are very

limited images for a profound and unfathomable mystery, but I believe they bring us closer to understanding it.

## Discernment

This is why discernment is so important. The difference between good and evil is pretty clear. There's not much to discern. We know we have to avoid evil; that is *synderesis.* But *between one good and another good, discernment is necessary: What is it that the Lord wants to do in me?* Or *Do I need to speak with this person or speak with that person?* There is no moral rule that tells me what to do, but the Lord wants to do something through me. He either wants me to speak with one person and not the other, or to speak with both of them.

Discernment is the capacity to open the floodgates, to let the water flow, and to see where it goes. When water flows, it follows a path. Where does the water of the Spirit flow? Where does the Lord want to take me? That is discernment.

There are interior and exterior methods of discernment. Interior discernment might ask these types of questions: If I do this, what fruit will it bear? Do I feel at peace about this? When I pray, what do I sense that Christ wants to do in me? Using exterior discernment, we might ask: What does the Word of God say? What do the constitutions of the Saint John Society say? What do my superiors say? What does the bishop say? What does my spiritual director say? What does the Church teach? These questions help me discern where the water is headed in each situation.

Over time, we learn to do this rapidly. Eventually, we learn that we don't need to get out a graphing calculator in order to make these decisions because the more we discern, the more natural it becomes. The Lord teaches us the attitudes that he wants us to have, because *he speaks in us. He doesn't play hide and seek; rather, he draws us toward him.*

Sometimes this impulse toward Christ's grace brings us to die to ourselves, to our old self. This process is not always like the water that flows serenely through the canals into the fields. Sometimes we encounter Iguazú Falls;[21] we are confronted with giant leaps, with ruptures, with death and resurrection. St. Paul often speaks of "disciplin[ing] my body,"[22] by which he means his old self. He speaks of *chastising myself so that Christ lives in me.* Why? Because we experience resistance to Christ's grace.

*There can be no holiness in Christ without suffering, without the cross.* Because of the flaws in our old selves, the fields that need to be irrigated in us are not always fertile land. Often times I have to use a pick and shovel so that the water can enter. There is a death in this because I am selfish, I'm carnal, I'm an opportunist, I'm arrogant, I'm proud, I'm lazy, I'm vain. . . . In order that all may be transformed in Christ, sometimes we need to be broken, to go through crosses and sufferings, to take leaps and to force ourselves a little. On the path to holiness, not everything is peaceful.

## The Beatitudes

Let's look at the Beatitudes.

The Beatitudes are the introduction to the Sermon on

---

21   Largest waterfall system in the world on the border of Argentina.
22   1 Cor 9:27.

the Mount: they are an anticipation of what will be said in the following chapters.

Blessed are the poor in spirit, those who mourn, the meek, those who hunger and thirst for righteousness, the merciful, the pure of heart, the peacemakers, those who are persecuted . . . Blessed are you, for your reward will be great in heaven.

We know that the Beatitudes reveal the character of Christ himself. The *Catechism of the Catholic Church* says, "The Beatitudes depict the countenance of Jesus Christ and portray his charity. They express the vocation of the faithful associated with the glory of his Passion and Resurrection; they shed light on the actions and attitudes characteristic of the Christian life; they are the paradoxical promises that sustain hope in the midst of tribulations; they proclaim the blessings and rewards already secured, however dimly, for Christ's disciples; they have begun in the lives of the Virgin Mary and all the saints."[23] If you re-read this quote, you'll notice that six facets of the Beatitudes are mentioned in one paragraph!

Before this retreat, I asked you each to choose one Beatitude out of the list and send me a reflection on it. Here is one of the responses I received:

> "Blessed are those who are poor in spirit for theirs is the kingdom of heaven." He who is poor in spirit knows that everything he has received has been given to him and, knowing how poor he is, rejoices to have been given such gifts. At the same time, he does not get attached to things and trusts in the Father, so he knows how to live joyfully, both in abundance and in scarcity. He knows how to suffer hunger,

---

[23]    CCC 1717.

cold, nakedness, and tiredness without losing his joy. He also knows how to value things, taking care of them and using them properly. Having the soul of a poor man, he knows that his ultimate good is not found in any material or created thing, but only in the Lord. The Lord is his only good: seek first the Kingdom of God. This Beatitude has touched me personally.

## Exercise

Now I'm going to propose some spiritual exercises for you:

1. The first is that you take the Gospel of John 15:1–11 and contemplate the vine and the branches. Do a prayerful reading of this text, reading slowly and pronouncing the words: "He who remains in me and I in him will bear much fruit." Use your imagination and your feelings to enter into these words.

   Ask for the grace to remain always in Christ, grafted to him. Give thanks for the call to be his disciple, to climb the mountain, to sit down and listen to his word, united to him, not only exteriorly, but also interiorly.

   You can also meditate on the Hymn of Philippians. Chapter 2 says, "Have among yourselves the same *attitude* that is also yours in Christ Jesus." In Greek, the word that is translated as "attitude" is *froneite,* which comes from *fren,* alluding to the mind. And "mind" in Greek means reason, will, and feelings of the heart; it combines all three ideas. This passage could also have been translated, "Have the same mentality as Christ Jesus." But "mentality" sounds very rational to us, right? This means more than that; it includes mentality and feelings and heart. It has the same meaning as "ethos"; the same heart, you could say, but there isn't an exact word for it. Maybe "heart" sounds too sentimental. The Bible *Libro del Pueblo de Dios* translates it "sentiments."

But I don't like the word "sentiments" very much. "Have the same sentiments" does a poor job of translating the meaning behind the word. I would prefer: "Have the same vision, the same rationality." I don't know how it could be said best, but the original word *froneite* includes all of this.

This "attitude" is the result of life in Christ: we begin to share his same attitude. Later on, in the Hymn of Philippians, St. Paul describes it: "He, though he was in the form of God, did not regard equality with God something to be grasped. Rather, he emptied himself, taking the form of a slave, coming in human likeness; and found human in appearance, he humbled himself, becoming obedient to death, even death on a cross. Because of this God greatly exalted him."[24] In some way, if we want to have the same mentality as Christ Jesus, our life has to be a parable, a copy of this hymn.

After the hymn, St. Paul explains this work of salvation a little more: I have been invited to be part of this vine, I have been grafted onto Christ, I have been saved, not through my choosing, but rather through God's design and his unconditional love. I can say, "I, Iván, have been personally called by Christ Jesus.

---

[24]    Phil 2:5ff.

In his providence, God loved me, and he called me. He called me personally."

The other day, I read a quote from Benedict XVI that said, "Faith is believing in this love of God."[25] It moved me deeply! This phrase alone, this simple phrase that I have heard a thousand times, moved me because it is the truth: I have to have faith in the love of God, that God loves me and *calls me to be grafted onto his Son, to live in the heart of Christ.* He rescued me from where I was and put me into the heart of his Son; he grafted me onto Christ to give me a new life.

And not only that! He called me to be a priest; he called me to be the image of his Son so that he might be the firstborn of many brothers.[26] This same idea is in Colossians.[27] Jesus wants to be the first-born of many, through each priest's surrendered life. The first of how many? How many will each one save? A thousand souls, says one book.[28] Each priest, throughout his life, will influence at least a thousand people . . . and I believe many more. Christ wants to be the firstborn among a thousand, at the very least. But in order to be the firstborn, he needs us to die so that he can live in us.

---

[25]   Pope Benedict XVI, "The Year of Faith. What is Faith?" General Audience, October 24, 2012.

[26]   See Rom 8:29.

[27]   See Col 1:15–20.

[28]   Brett Brannen, *To Save a Thousand Souls: A Guide to Discerning Diocesan Priesthood.* Valdosta: Vianney Vocations, 2010.

2. As a second spiritual exercise, take Galatians 2:20, when St. Paul says, "Yet I live, no longer I, but Christ lives in me." Before this he says, "I have been crucified with Christ. . . . Insofar as I now live in the flesh, I live by faith in the son of God who has loved me and given himself up for me." How powerful this is! "Yet I live, no longer I, but Christ lives in me." Let us ask for the grace to be able to have this phrase of St. Paul incarnate in ourselves.

We have been made a new being, as St. Paul says, "Whoever is in Christ is a new creation; the old things have passed away."[29] The old has passed away. *Being willing to let go of that old identity isn't so easy, but now there is something new in me: Christ in me.* St. Paul says, "Even if we once knew Christ according to the flesh, yet now we know him so no longer."[30] *This isn't a contemplation on Christ's long-ago life; this is something new that is in me.*

Therefore, let's focus on detecting the signs that we are becoming more alive in Christ. Let's try to pinpoint them: Are there impulses in me that don't come naturally? In other words, do I see attitudes that are not from myself but rather from Christ who lives in me?

Is there something that has broken through my normal habits? Or do I continue to be my old self? Do I recognize things about which I could say, for example: *This isn't Marcos; this is Christ in Marcos.*

---

[29]    2 Cor 5:17.

[30]    2 Cor 5:16.

*Because Marcos would never have done such a thing, never would have taken that step.* I'm sure there are! Where are the places where you no longer recognize the old self, but rather see the new self in Christ Jesus? What are the steps that you have taken, even at the price of renouncing old values, including good ones, that have unbalanced the whole?

When you are growing in the spiritual life, you begin to realize that there are things that are good but which no longer fit in your life: they've already passed; they are old. And in Christ these things have no place. Even though they are good in themselves, they just don't fit.

When you grow spiritually, your life begins to be unified. If you are intellectual, affectionate, efficient, private, hyperactive, calm—no matter what you are like, you will come to discover new qualities in yourself. For example, if you are very intellectual, maybe you will discover an interest in action that wasn't in you before and realize that it comes from Christ. If you have trouble concentrating, you will begin to have an interest in reflection that doesn't come from you but rather from Christ in you, etc. And so the whole person comes to be balanced in a new "ethos" that is from Christ.

I often see this happen in seminarians: *How much this person has grown! He is becoming well-rounded where he was lacking something before! And the virtues he already had, he is increasing and growing.* Or sometimes you see that this is not the case, that the person is going backwards, that there is little fruit because he isn't advancing. This can have many different causes.

Our lives begin to be unified. This is a sign of living in Christ, above all for those of us who are trying to follow him literally.

The other day I watched the Argentinian national team play a soccer match with a few other priests. The truth is that we didn't care too much about the match: it was fun to watch and relax a little, but we have lost interest in soccer. If we had been going crazy about the game two days beforehand, as some of us would have in the past, that would have been a bad sign, a sign that we were not coming to be unified in Christ, that our interests were not becoming more Christlike. In the end, we did go to watch it, but if we hadn't been able to, no one would have been very upset. That is a good sign that we are growing in unity in Christ. Our love for Jesus and our trust in him continues to grow.

Some time ago, Sister Bernadette, in our sister order of the Society of Mary, said, "When someone says, 'Jesus, I trust in you,' he is also saying, 'Jesus, united to you I trust in the Father.'" It's like saying: *Grafted onto you, Jesus, I entrust myself to God, I entrust myself to the Father.* And that is an excellent way of growing in prayer.

3.   In the third place, I propose reading through the Beatitudes and asking Jesus to help us see ourselves in them and to contemplate his face through them. *Lord, how did you mourn?* etc. You can go to other passages of

the Bible to help you with this. For example, if you are meditating on Christ mourning, you can spiritually place yourself before Jesus on the cross. *Lord, how were you a peacemaker?* And I can go to another passage of the Gospel that suggests itself for my meditation. *How did you hunger and thirst for righteousness? How were you pure of heart?*

4.  Finally, meditate on the Our Father, which is the heart of the Sermon on the Mount. Jesus teaches us to pray and live as sons and daughters of the Father. Only then can we understand the Sermon on the Mount. Meditate on the Our Father, praying it slowly. For example, say, *Our Father,* and stop for a moment. Pray with your heart, be silent, then repeat the words. Those who know how can pray in tongues between the different petitions so that it reaches deeper into your soul. Then continue: *Who art in heaven . . . ; hallowed be thy name . . . ; Thy kingdom come . . .*

*Glory be to the Father, and to the Son, and to the Holy Spirit. As it was in the beginning, is now, and ever shall be, world without end. Amen.*

# BLESSED ARE THE POOR: INTRODUCTION

BEFORE we look at the first Beatitude—"Blessed are the poor in spirit"—it's important to note that the Beatitudes are the introduction to the Sermon on the Mount and that they have three parts.

The first part of each Beatitude is the proclamation "happy" or "blessed"—"*macarios*" in Greek—which is an observation: "Blessed are you if this or that happens."

You can say, in some sense, "Blessed are you now." The recompense is in the future, but the observation is in the present: "Blessed are those who are like this." In some way, the happiness or blessedness of the future world that Jesus promises makes itself present in us believers already, here and now, although it's not yet fully realized. But we already have the initial down payment for that future blessedness.

Saint Thomas Aquinas says:

> Expounders of Holy Scripture are not agreed in speaking of these rewards [of the Beatitudes]. For some, with Ambrose, hold that all these rewards refer to the life to come; while Augustine holds them to refer to the present life; and Chrysostom in his homilies says that some refer to the future, and some to the present life. In order to make the matter clear we must take note that hope of future happiness may be in us for two reasons. First, by reason of our having a preparation for, or a disposition to future happiness; and this is by way of merit; secondly, by a kind of imperfect inchoation of future happiness in holy men, even in this life. For it is one thing

to hope that the tree will bear fruit, when the leaves begin to appear, and another, when we see the first signs of the fruit.[1]

This first hope for future happiness is the one we have in faith: we know that God will reward us abundantly "by way of merit." And the second reason for hope comes from our ability to enjoy the first fruits of happiness in this life because the Beatitudes carry their own reward, in some way. When we begin to live the Beatitudes, we receive the joy that is intrinsically in them.

There are two ways of being happy: as a hope for joy to come and also as anticipation of future joy, but where happiness is already taking place or is already beginning to be lived now, in some way or another.

Sometimes we use these types of expressions when we speak to someone: *How great that you get a vacation,* or *How lucky you are that you have good credit*, which means, *What's happening to you is so good.* The Beatitudes are saying the same thing: they point out what happens when we truly live them, and they also promise happiness for the future.

The second part of each Beatitude is their content:. . . *the poor in spirit; . . . the meek; . . . those who mourn*; etc. They draw an image of Christ and of the Christian.

The third part of each Beatitude is the reason: *for . . . They shall inherit the earth. They will be consoled. They will be satisfied. They will obtain mercy. They shall see God. They will be called children of God. The Kingdom of Heaven is theirs.*

These are our reasons for being happy. As we have been

[1]    I–II, q.69, a.2.

saying, many of the Beatitudes are formulated in the future but already in some way begin to be lived now.

Let's turn now to the first of the Beatitudes: "Blessed are the poor in spirit, for the Kingdom of Heaven is theirs." The Spanish translation in *El Libro del Pueblo de Dios* says: "Happy are those who have the *soul of the poor* because theirs is the Kingdom of Heaven."[2]

This Beatitude isn't formulated for the future. It is expressed in the present: it says that the kingdom of heaven belongs already—here and now—to those who are poor in spirit. The "Kingdom of Heaven" in Matthew is the same as the kingdom of God, or, as we call it, the "New Situation in Christ."

*The poor in spirit are those who live in the New Situation, the New Situation is theirs.* They can already live as children of the Father, as brothers and sisters of others, completely dedicated to a mission and already experiencing the salvation of God in their lives. *They are poor, they are emptied of themselves.*

## What the Beatitude Is Not

Let's consider what this Beatitude is not.

First and foremost, it is *not* an invitation to resign ourselves to the existence of poverty. *If the poor are happy and blessed, well, let them stay poor. Why take them out of that happiness?* That would be a very absurd and simplistic way of understanding this Beatitude, but at times Christianity has been accused of this view.

---

2     Mt 5:3.

There is a Marxist accusation that Christianity, promising future goods, invites people to a present resignation,
above all toward the poor. It claims that Christianity has
historically tried to placate the poor with these promises
about the future. But that is simply not true. It's not true
either historically or in our daily experiences. The Church
goes out to the peripheries, day after day, educating, healing, forming, taking care of the poor. . . . But this is the
beginning of a different discussion.

This Beatitude is also not an invitation merely to change
our state in life, as if it wanted to say that the poorer we are
now, the better, because we will be rewarded more in the
kingdom of heaven.

On the contrary, the social teaching of the popes speaks
of the importance of the transformation of social condi-
tions, of the need for structural changes, and of our responsibility to be involved in the fight against poverty. All of this
makes it clear to us that an essential part of the Christian
vocation, especially the lay Christian, is working for a more
just world.

In *Laudato Sì*, Pope Francis shows a great sensitivity to
the suffering of the poor. He says, "Nowadays, for example, we are conscious of the disproportionate and unruly
growth of many cities, which have become unhealthy to
live in, not only because of pollution caused by toxic emis-
sions but also as a result of urban chaos, poor transporta-
tion, and visual pollution, and noise."[3]

The pope is from Buenos Aires, so he knows what he is
talking about. We also share that experience. At times when

---

[3]    LS 44.

we are walking through the slums, the poverty is almost inconceivable. It's painful to see the chaos of the people—how they have to commute in those trains, those buses, so many hours each day. Poor people suffer many things that are so unhealthy.

The encyclical continues, "Many cities are huge, inefficient structures, excessively wasteful of energy and water. Neighborhoods, even those recently built, are congested, chaotic and lacking in sufficient green space. We were not meant to be inundated by cement, asphalt, glass and metal, and deprived of physical contact with nature."[4] And later it says, "Frequently, we find beautiful and carefully manicured green spaces in so-called 'safer' areas of cities, but not in the more hidden areas where the disposable of society live."[5] The beautiful physical spaces are ordinarily associated with material wealth, while the poor generally live in places that are ugly and sordid; that is how it is.

This is all to say that the fight against poverty is a preoccupation of the Church: we are fighting for a more just world, where those that don't have a voice can be heard and the condition of their life matters.

## Jesus Identifies Himself With the Poor

Having said that, we must recognize that in this Beatitude—as in all of them—there are two levels of interpretation: the first is the more material level, and the second is a more spiritual level. In fact, the parallel Beatitude in Luke's

---

[4]    LS 44.
[5]    LS 45.

Gospel doesn't say "poor in spirit" but rather "the poor"[6] directly.

And this more material level seems to me to be very important because, although it isn't an invitation to resignation, Jesus makes it clear that he knows the misery and the difficulties of the poor and of those who suffer, and that their situation isn't outside the providence nor the recompense of God.

This is meant to be a comfort in the struggle. God doesn't want anyone to be materially poor—poor as we understand that here in Latin America: excluded, marginalized, without access to education, to culture, to the goods of human dignity. That goes against the plan of God. What this Beatitude is saying is that God knows material poverty and that he will compensate those who live in poverty; it will be taken into account.

For example, there is the parable of Lazarus and the rich man. Why does Lazarus go to heaven? Because he had suffered much, which is what Jesus said in the parable: "Lazarus likewise received what was bad."[7] Very well, now he is repaid.

In contrast, *the rich man doesn't go to heaven, not because he wasn't poor, but rather because he was insensitive. The poor go to heaven for being poor;* there is a divine distributive justice. God sees and pays attention: there is nothing that escapes God's attention.

The other level of all the Beatitudes—but especially of this one—is the spiritual level. This Beatitude is a freely

---

[6]     Lk 6:20.
[7]     Lk 16:25.

chosen path for a greater configuration with Christ because he decided to live in poverty. This is the Beatitude's most spiritual and most positive sense. Christ lived in poverty, but he was not marginalized. He had access to a good education, had social grace, and a sense of belonging. He was a worker, but he wasn't discriminated against because of it.

I think that both the material and spiritual meanings are important here, and we need to keep them both in mind in order to fully understand the Beatitudes. The material meaning acts like a balm, consoling us in times of poverty and sufferings that we don't choose in our lives or in the lives of those around us. And the spiritual meaning shows us an ideal for our life, something we can freely choose.

# BLESSED ARE THE POOR: PART 1

## The Material Aspect of This Beatitude

THE first meaning is especially important for us as priests. We encounter the poor in our daily ministry and apostolate, and it is essential that we have that vision of Jesus: to have his preferential love for the poor and to know that they have an equalizing hope in Christ.

Jesus identifies himself with the poor: he knows them well, knows their poverty, moves about comfortably among them, and speaks about them many times. He experienced in his own flesh the exclusion of the lepers, the contempt of the sinners, the excommunication of the Samaritans, the loneliness of the prisoners and the sick, the cold of the naked, the thirst of the vagabonds, the hunger of the unemployed.

And he noticed them.

For example, in that parable where Jesus says: *I am like that landowner who goes out to hire those who are unemployed in the morning, at midday, and in the afternoon.*[1] Christ noticed the unemployed youth that were there, wasting time. Sometimes, when you go to some neighborhoods, the group of unemployed youth drinking beer on the corner catches your attention, and you ask yourself: *What are*

---

[1] See Mt 20:1–16.

*these kids doing here, on a weekday, at 10:00 am, sitting around drinking beer?* And it pains you, it moves you.

That is how Jesus thinks of these parables: first he sees and lives the circumstances that he describes in them. In other words, Christ saw those young men hanging out in the plaza. And he saw the sower that went out to sow and work in the fields, and the poor widow who with one coin gave all that she had to live on.

And that is why he identified himself with them. This text of the Gospel is the inspirational text for the Cenacle program[2]: "For I was hungry, and you gave me food, I was thirsty and you gave me drink, a stranger and you welcomed me, naked and you clothed me, ill and you cared for me, in prison and you visited me."[3] *When, Lord? When did we do that?* They asked him in the parable. And he responded, "Whatever you did for one of these least brothers of mine, you did for me."[4]

He identifies himself with the poor, as if he were to say: *Service to the poor is service to me, because I identify myself with them.* And precisely because he knows that suffering, he announces this Good News: *The Father doesn't forget you. Take heart, blessed ones! Because your suffering will be repaid, will be taken into account.*

Jesus wasn't a social activist. You never hear him speak against the Romans or against the social structures of his era. He didn't say anything about slavery, for example; he

---

[2]   The Saint John Society's program of New Evangelization for high school students, which focuses on the works of mercy.

[3]   Mt 25:35–36.

[4]   Mt 25:44–45.

didn't go into it. But *he touched the heart of mankind and that is why his message revolutionized the social structure.*

Many of you have lived for a while in Serrezuela[5] and have worked with the people who are the poorest. You know their poverty. And you know that *Jesus lives in you, the resurrected Jesus lives in you. He gives you a love for the poor and a desire to be with them, a desire which needs to be nourished.*

### The Feelings of the Good Shepherd

Some time ago, one of the priests of the SSJ wrote to me: "Ever since the VAE retreat,[6] I have been able to experience a stronger reality than in other circumstances or situations. That is to say, it has become a lived reality: I am the same as them. They can be my friends. It's not that I didn't believe this before. Even when Fr. Christian would say it, I'd think, 'Of course, that's obvious,' but experiencing it is interesting. One of them began to go to Alcoholics Anonymous. I take him every Tuesday, and I go to visit him so that he doesn't get back into drink or drugs; I invite him to come over in the afternoon because that is the time that they invite him to the bad parties." These are the feelings of the good shepherd.

That is why this Beatitude is very connected to the bond of fraternity: in Christ we are brothers and sisters. *The New Situation that Christ creates makes it possible for you to feel*

---

[5]   A small town on the outskirts of the province of Córdoba, Argentina.

[6]   An evangelization retreat run by the Saint John Society for the poor from rural areas or from the slums of large cities. *Volver a Empezar* is also our program of evangelization for the poor.

*and to live as a brother or sister of others who are different from you.* The one who becomes poor in spirit can experience the poorest of the poor as brothers and sisters. And the inverse is true as well: the one who experiences that the poor person is his brother becomes poorer in spirit in Christ.

It seems to me that this is part of our life, part of the beauty of our life in the Saint John Society and of our particular charism: to be able to announce the New Situation in Christ with deeds and words to the poor also.

Recently we spoke about this together, about our work with the poor and how it is always a challenge to be able to dedicate the necessary time to the poorest, and about the importance of the work we do with them. And we challenged ourselves to remain vigilant in this work.

A while back, speaking about this with Juan who is one of the missionaries, I realized that the *Volver a Empezar* program in Pilar[7] is the only program in which all of the SSJ priests work. He reminded me that "in the rest of our programs, one man works in Legatus,[8] another in Cenacle, but in *Volver a Empezar,* we are all there, we are all involved."

## It Is Not an Easy Task

Thanks be to God, our mission is growing, and its fruits are part of the beauty of this life. Nevertheless, we have to recognize there is difficulty in maintaining a balance between two worlds: the world of the college students we also work

---

[7]    A suburb of Buenos Aires.
[8]    Legatus is the Saint John Society's program of New Evangelization for professional men.

with and the world of the most impoverished. It is not an easy task, and it requires a particular personality, but it is an intrinsic part of the Saint John Society. From the beginning, we have had this sense of belonging to two different worlds.

I think that the Ministry of Unity discussed in our constitutions, which unites these two disparate worlds in our work, is novel and has great power for evangelization.

That is why I invite us to contemplate this work we are doing in this apostolate and to ask Christ for an even greater love for the poor. I know you already have this love, but ask for an even greater love. And be proud of this work! How important it is to be able to offer a program that is exclusively for evangelization in these neighborhoods, one that announces a life in Christ to the poorest!

We have this certainty: that we also announce the Good News to them with zeal, and that it is especially in the poor where the Good News is manifested with the most power. We hold this certainty proper to our charism.

And in addition, think about our approach, our method for doing this. It is impressive to see how the San Juan Diego program[9] in the United States has grown and how it transforms the lives of its members. And the Volver a Empezar program in Argentina, it seems to me, also continues to grow. As does the work in the prison in Córdoba, just recently begun, which I am sure will go well, with the help of God.

Why don't we dedicate ourselves to the material aid of

---

[9]    A program of New Evangelization for Hispanic immigrants in the US run by the Saint John Society.

the poor also? Because we want to focus on giving them something which can only come from the Church.

It's not easy, because their situation pains us and calls out for action. But our closeness to them happens only by offering them something even more necessary than material aid, even more important, something harder to find than material goods, and that is *this proclamation of the New Life in Christ.*

The evangelicals do it: they draw near to the poorest people with their evangelizing proclamation. And even though they don't have all the spiritual, doctrinal, and devotional means that we have in the Catholic Church, they are very clear about what they have to offer. It's like Peter in the Acts of the Apostles: "I have neither silver nor gold, but what I do have I give you: in the name of Jesus Christ the Nazorean, rise and walk."[10]

And the power of transformation that this proclamation carries is immense. I think that within the Catholic Church, at least in the experience that I have, which is small and limited, there is a novelty in this. It is a certainty that has grown weak, but which still comprises the nucleus of our identity and mission.

### Exercise

Let us meditate on what we've discussed up to this point.

1.  For prayer, take this Beatitude and contemplate Jesus as poor, in both the material and spiritual sense. Jesus who was born poor, who lived as a poor man and who

---

[10]    Acts 3:6.

died poor. Jesus whose food is to do the will of the Father and carry out his work. Where is the treasure of Jesus? What is his relationship with money? Contemplate him.

2. Next, meditate on what the statutes of the Saint John the Apostle Association say about the work among the most poor and our particular style of work that we have with them. Look also at the reasons for which we want to dedicate ourselves to the poor:

"In recent years, the Catholic Church has been losing its evangelizing presence in this sector of society, watching the communities of evangelical churches, and even other sects, grow and prosper. Thousands of baptized Catholics are evangelized by Christian churches of various denominations that have multiplied due to their intense missionary labor in these places."

"Due to this, many people have stopped practicing their Catholic faith and many others have changed to other Christian denominations, if not to other religions or sects."

"*The difficulty is of reaching them with a compelling evangelizing method whose characteristics are suitable for the people who make up this broad social sector.* Without a doubt, this task demands the dedication of time and energy. And it is sufficiently challenging so as to demand a specific dedication, with its proper modalities and style of work."

"In response to this need and in communion with many of the initiatives that have arisen for the New

Evangelization in this social sector, the 'Saint Joseph Branch' [of the SSJ] seeks to be a contribution to this pastoral work of the Catholic Church. Preaching the Good News to the poor is one of the clearest signs of the presence of Christ in the Church."[11]

Remember when John the Baptist asked Jesus: "Are you the one who is to come or should we look for another?" And Jesus responds with an eloquent sign: "The blind regain their sight, the lame walk, lepers are cleansed, the deaf hear, the dead are raised, and *the poor have the Good News proclaimed to them.*"[12]

"That is why the Saint Joseph Branch seeks among the humblest, those who are the most marginalized, and encourages them to find their place as baptized persons in the local Church."[13]

3.  In the third place, look at the impact of Christ's teaching in you. What attitudes and desires do these passages stir up in you? Do you feel yourself identifying with this mission? How can you grow in it?

Think about the poor people that you know or have met. Imagine their faces one after the other. What does proclaiming this Beatitude demand of you? What sort of person do you have to be in order

---

[11] Statutes ASJA, 21. *The Aparecida Document also* says in #100: "In the last decades, we see with preoccupation, that on the one hand, there are numerous persons who lose the transcendent meaning of their lives and abandon religious practices, and, on the other hand, there are a significant number of Catholics abandoning the Church to go to other religious groups."

[12] Mt 11:3–5.

[13] Statutes ASJA, 21.

to announce the Good News of the kingdom to someone who is poor?

Finally, to sum it all up:

First, contemplate Jesus who is poor, who lives among the poor, who preaches among the poor, who loves the poor, and who identifies himself with them. There are hundreds of passages that you could use.

Next, contemplate our mission among the poor and see: What does this demand of you? Do you have a love for it? Do you take pride in this mission? How is your commitment, your dedication to it? Use the passages quoted above to help you with this.

*Glory be to the Father, and to the Son, and to the Holy Spirit. As it was in the beginning, is now, and ever shall be, world without end. Amen.*

# BLESSED ARE THE POOR: PART 2

## The Spiritual Aspect of This Beatitude

NOW let's look at the second meaning of the phrase "Blessed are the poor in spirit."

This second meaning looks at the more spiritual aspect of the Beatitude. We've already talked about how the first meaning is more material, that it has to do with being able to see the poor with the gaze of Jesus and that it touches a more apostolic aspect: contemplating our work among the poor.

This second meaning consists in seeing ourselves as someone who has been called to live the Beatitudes by radically following Jesus Christ.

*Only someone who becomes poor, meek, suffering, and merciful can experience in his or her own life the life of Christ. Also, only the one who follows Christ radically comes to experience the spiritual meaning of the Beatitudes.*

The poverty that Jesus speaks about in this Beatitude isn't material poverty alone but incorporates an ethical and religious dimension. Above all, to be "poor in spirit" is a spiritual disposition. It encapsulates the concept of the poor found in the Old Testament. The poor are the humble who entrust themselves to God, who put their trust in him, who live out the Covenant and do not trust in their chariots and horses.

They are the poor of Yahweh; they are humble of heart, they live simply. For example: "I will leave as a remnant in your midst a people humble and lowly, who shall take refuge in the name of the LORD; the remnant of Israel. They shall do no wrong and speak no lies; nor shall there be found in their mouths a deceitful tongue; they shall pasture and couch their flocks with none to disturb them."[1]

## Our Treasure

There are two passages in the same Sermon on the Mount that illuminate this Beatitude—or the meaning of this Beatitude—with great clarity.

One is Matthew 6:19–21: "Do not store up for yourselves treasures on earth, where moth and decay destroy, and thieves break in and steal. But store up treasures in heaven, where neither moth nor decay destroys, nor thieves break in and steal. For where your treasure is, there also will your heart be." This passage enlarges the Beatitude and helps explain it.

*Our treasure isn't in goods, or in possessions, or in glory, or in honor; rather, it is in heaven: in living before the eyes of God, in doing the will of the Father, and in carrying out his work. And as that is where our treasure is, there also will our heart be.*

Matthew 6:24 says the same thing, when Jesus says, "No one can serve two masters. He will either hate one and love the other, or be devoted to one and despise the other. You cannot serve God and mammon."

---

[1]    Zep 3:12–13.

You cannot serve God and mammon, God and money, God and your own glory, God and your own comfort, God and your fame, or God and your own success. Money is a symbol of the search for one's own wellbeing. It is impossible to serve both. One will be valued in detriment to the other.

Thus, someone who is poor in spirit in this sense is someone who makes Christ and his kingdom his own treasure. It is a poverty of spirit that permits you to serve God with your whole heart.

That is why I think that the more you grow in your formation and your desire to follow Jesus, your priestly apostolic life entails a renunciation of human projects that in themselves are good, but that aren't as fully oriented toward your life's mission as priests of the New Evangelization. There are good things to which you naturally aspire or would aspire but that we renounce in this life that we choose in order to serve God with more freedom.

We have a project—personal, yet shared in common—that is very great, very ambitious, very comprehensive, for which we renounce other, lesser projects.

### "Lord, Count on Me for Whatever You Want"

In regard to your personal projects and aspirations, it seems to me that it is good to say to the Lord: *Lord, I don't want to be attached to anything, to any riches of this world.*

*I don't want to prefer one place to another; I don't want to get attached. I want to serve you with total radicality, and to announce your kingdom to the poor, to the lowly, to youth, and to students. Count on me for whatever you want.* That is the true poverty of spirit in this life.

The one who is poor in spirit is free.

So I ask you: do you have any riches that you still don't want to sell? Maybe you have deep aspirations: success, recognition, glory, esteem (I don't believe any of you are seeking money; we already know that aspiration isn't ours).

But . . . might there be some other thing to which you are attached?

Because the one who is poor in spirit is free, is simple; he lives before God. In contrast, the one who doesn't live before God, lives caught up in other expectations or other projects. Are there deep-rooted goals which you realize you still haven't renounced?

And the little things . . .

Are you attached to anything that diminishes your freedom? Some material good? Some electronic gadget? Some piece of clothing? I don't know . . . some little thing that you realize reduces your freedom.

It's such a positive thing to be able to live an austere lifestyle, and also so liberating.

Among the reflections that you sent me before this retreat, I read: "I would like to begin commenting on the Beatitude that most resonated with me: 'Blessed are the poor in spirit for theirs in the Kingdom of Heaven.' The one who is poor in spirit knows that all that he has is given to him, that he has received everything gratuitously, and knowing himself poor, he rejoices to receive a gift. On the other hand, he doesn't get attached to things, but trusts in the Father, and that is why he can live with so much joy, in abundance as in scarcity. He knows how to suffer hunger, cold, nakedness, and tiredness without losing heart. He also knows how to value things, care for them, and use them as he ought. Because he is poor in spirit, he knows that his true good isn't anything material or created, but rather that it is the Lord. The Lord is his only good; he seeks first the Kingdom. This Beatitude has touched me personally."

Notice the three interesting things that it says: The Lord is my kingdom and my treasure. I am generous and detached; I know how to care for and properly value things. Therefore, I am grateful because I value everything as a gift.

For example, if I am in a house that doesn't have heating, but we are able to hold our retreat there, and I am able to have my own room in which to pray . . . Well, I give thanks for all these things! I receive it all as a poor person would. I don't devalue it, but rather accept it with gratitude. And when something is lacking . . . well, it's lacking. I also know how to accept that with simplicity.

In another one of your mediations there is a similar reference: "It is Good News to recognize yourself poor before God, to be able to connect more deeply with Him. I am thinking about interior poverty, that is to say, the capacity to recognize ourselves—through this virtue—exactly as we are before God: poor and in need of him. Humility carries with it simplicity and poverty of spirit; that is why, as the Psalm says, God resists the proud and looks upon the humble. It is good news because I know that if I am humble and live out poverty, I am more detached from the world and from myself in order to enjoy heavenly goods."

## Doesn't Seek so Much for Self

It follows that poverty of spirit is tied to humility and to interior liberty. Someone who is poor in spirit doesn't seek much; he has simplicity. He seeks to serve often, to minister to others, to love deeply, and to devote himself to others, but he doesn't seek much for himself. He is detached and lives with interior liberty.

For example, it's good to be detached from the grades we receive. Of course we need to study and learn, but we can exercise detachment from our grades, from recognitions, from positions, from what we think belongs to us. We can seek to be humble and detached and to center ourselves time after time on serving Christ and others: that is our treasure. That is why it's not poverty of spirit to be detached only from material things, since that is only one aspect of it; rather, we must also be detached from ourselves.

There is also a pseudo-poverty of spirit, which is the detachment of the rich person. The rich man is detached because he knows he will continue to have. So we see some young people from comfortable backgrounds that don't take care of things because they know that if they break something, they will get a replacement. They have never lacked anything and don't value what they have, which, since they are careless with what they have, is a sort of bourgeois entitlement.

## Poverty of Spirit

We don't have to go to extremes to be poor in spirit. We don't have to have a puritanical or negative vision of material goods or of money. Our poverty of spirit should include caring for and valuing things. Father Pablo is always pointing this out: "Let's take care of things; let's be austere. Let's value material goods like the poor do."

In addition, in our life we are going to have to manage money and administer it, precisely because the more people we serve, the more material goods we must also work with. Just look at the Pastoral Center in Pilar.[2] In order to build it, we needed to manage of a lot of money, which included organizing fundraising events, asking for donations, and administering resources. That is to say, our poverty includes the capacity to manage material goods with responsibility, with gratitude, and with poverty of spirit.

This is an important aspect because we are not talking about *the disinterested poverty of an adolescent.* Each of you is being formed with the capacity to manage money for the glory of God, remaining poor in spirit yourselves. You can begin to cultivate this habit now, by caring for what we have and by responsibly and justly administering material goods.

What's certain in this Beatitude is that it is impossible for the heart to be empty. *The center of the heart will either be occupied by Jesus . . . or will be filled with things.*

### Exercise

1.  First, let us meditate on the poverty of Jesus and our apostolate with the poor. Our constitution says, "In his love for us, Christ, 'who although he was rich became

---

2    A center for SSJ programs outside of Buenos Aires.

poor'[3] and who came to proclaim 'the Good News to the poor,'[4] proclaims us happy if we imitate his poor life,[5] like workers who have no other interest besides that of serving their Lord."[6]

2. We can imitate his life by serving others and by embracing the most common domestic chores, which allows us to draw closer to the life of the poor. It's good to do these things authentically, not "putting up" with these services, but rather *embracing them* from the core of our identity. We find the capacity for this embrace within Christ's call to identify ourselves with the poorest and to identify ourselves with Christ himself, "who although he was rich became poor."

3. This second meditation is about our own poverty. How do we live this virtue of spiritual poverty in the context of the vocation that we have received?

   Meditate on God's promise of recompense, which is very reassuring: "Blessed are the poor in spirit, for theirs is the Kingdom of Heaven." Only he who is poor can receive the New Situation in Christ as something that really belongs to him. The kingdom belongs to the poor. It's that simple and certain. We cannot live as children of the Father, as brothers and sisters of one another, with the radicality of Jesus, if we are not poor in spirit.

---

[3]    2 Cor 8:9.
[4]    Lk 4:18.
[5]    Cf. Lk 6:20.
[6]    SSJ Constitutions, #34.

That is why Jesus says, "Seek first the Kingdom of God and his righteousness, and all these things will be given you besides."

*Radically living out of the New Life implies this spiritual poverty*, implies that we continue trying to obtain this virtue.

If I am poor, the kingdom of heaven belongs to me. Meditate on this belonging. The experience of the New Life in Christ, this New Situation, belongs to me.

*Glory be to the Father, and to the Son and to the Holy Spirit, as it was in the beginning, is now and ever shall be, world without end.*

# BLESSED ARE THE MEEK: PART 1

IN the New American Bible, the second Beatitude is translated as "Blessed are the meek for they will inherit the land." In the Spanish Bible, *El Libro del Pueblo de Dios*, the phrase that is used instead of "the meek" is *los pacientes*, or "those who are patient," which is also a valid translation of the Greek words in the original text. As I will explain, the concept of patience has a fuller meaning for this Beatitude.

In this Beatitude, we will look at three different meanings in the concept of patience: the first meaning is knowing how to suffer, the second is being able to wait, and the third is not getting irritated.

### Knowing How to Suffer

Patience expresses the New Situation of those who know Christ because it is in Jesus that we learn to suffer, we learn to wait, and we learn to be meek. I like the word "patient" more than "meek" for this Beatitude because the word "meek" alludes only to the third sense, that of not getting irritated, while the word "patient" includes the other two meanings. In fact, the word "patient" in the medical field also refers to someone who suffers.

Jesus taught the Beatitudes on the Mount of the Beatitudes. I once had the opportunity to celebrate Mass there. It is a beautiful place, in Galilee. There is a Church of the Beatitudes on one of the hills, where, according to tradition, Jesus first taught them. And the people look out at the whole Sea of Galilee behind the altar as the priest celebrates the Mass.

Jesus taught the Beatitudes on this mount of Galilee, but he put them into practice radically on Mount Calvary. *There on the cross, Jesus incarnated the Beatitudes to the greatest possible extent.* The crucified one, naked, hanging between heaven and earth . . .

He was never poorer than on the cross because there he had absolutely nothing, not even his Father, at least in his human experience. He was never more patient, because there he suffered in his body and in his soul with meekness, "like a lamb led to the slaughter," Isaiah writes;[1] he is "the Lamb that seemed to have been slain" of Revelation.[2]

He was never more afflicted because there he carried all the sin and suffering of the world. He was never more persecuted for practicing justice. He was just, but nevertheless was counted among evildoers. He was never more merciful: "Father, forgive them, they know not what they do."[3] With these words, Jesus broke open the flask of mercy and poured it out over the world.

He was never of a purer heart because there was no twisted intention that brought him to the cross. He was only moved by love for the Father and love of humanity. In the purity of Christ on the cross, there was nothing hidden. He was naked and exposed.

He was never a greater peacemaker than on the cross

---

[1]    Is 53:7.
[2]    Rv 5:6.
[3]    Lk 23:34.

because it is the cross that reconciles us with God and with one another. Christ "broke down the dividing wall of enmity"[4] (between Jews and pagans) Saint Paul writes, and "there is neither Jew nor Greek, there is neither slave nor free person, there is not male and female, for you are all one in Christ Jesus."[5] The cross is an eloquent and powerful sign of peace. When you are fighting with someone, look at the cross; you will see how it teaches you peace.

Never did Christ hunger and thirst more for righteousness than from the cross. "I have eagerly desired to eat this Passover with you,"[6] Jesus said, alluding to the cross. The Passover wasn't only the Last Supper, but rather also included the passion and the cross.

That is why the maximum point of descent is also the point of his ascent. *His apparent ignominy is his glory,* in reality. It is the triumph of the cross. We celebrate this triumph on September 14, the feast of the Exaltation of the Cross.

Christ made the cross a symbol of victory: the victory of the love of the crucified God over death and sin, over riches and power, over hatred, over vengeance, and over lust; that is, over everything that is in opposition to the Beatitudes.

It is the triumph of the cross over the *counter-beatitudes.*

## The Beatitudes of the World

We could formulate the beatitudes of the world like this:

Blessed are the rich.

---

[4] Eph 2:14.
[5] Gal 3:28.
[6] Lk 22:15.

Blessed are the powerful.
Blessed are those who don't have to wait.
Blessed are those who avoid all suffering.
Blessed are the self-serving (instead of those who hunger and
    thirst for justice).
Blessed are the hard, the avenging.
Blessed are the lustful.
Blessed are those who make war and win.

Jesus triumphs over the worldly beatitudes. On the cross, he triumphs over these counter-beatitudes.

His apparent overthrow and weakness constitute his triumph. There is an image in the movie *The Passion of the Christ* directed by Mel Gibson that points toward this: when Jesus dies, one raindrop falls. It would appear that heaven cries for the death of the Son, but in that same instant of his apparent defeat, the devil shouts in desperation, becoming aware of the reality of the triumph of the cross. Satan's greatest apparent victory is in reality his greatest defeat, for the fidelity and merciful love of the Son redeem the world.

*The Beatitudes are paradoxes; we will never fully understand everything about them, just as the cross of Christ is paradoxical.*

Benedict XVI says, "Suffering is precisely the path of transformation; and without suffering, nothing is transformed."[7]

*Salvation doesn't come from suffering, it comes from love.* But in the historical context of the sin of man, love is

---

[7]    Pope Benedict XVI, Address to the Diocesan Clergy of Aosta, July 25, 2005, https://w2.vatican.va/content/benedict-xvi/en/speeches/2005/july/documents/hf_ben-xvi_spe_20050725_diocesi-aosta.html.

clothed in suffering. What saves us is the love of God, but that love is a crucified love.

## Man of Sorrows

We see that Jesus is a man of suffering: he is called "a man of sorrows."[8] We contemplate his suffering on the cross, to which we must always return, because the cross of Christ fills us with consolation. In his prayer, St. Ignatius says, "Passion of Christ, strengthen (or comfort) me." The passion of Christ comforts us.

But Jesus didn't only suffer on the cross, even though that was his greatest suffering.

He also *suffered in his poverty,* in the exile of his infancy, and in his loneliness, as a man who grew up and lived with such a mystery. His communion with his Father was his source of joy, but also a source of loneliness.

He suffered in his itinerant ministry; he suffered the incomprehension of his disciples. *He knew suffering in his own life. He also knew profound joy, too, but he is a man of sorrows.*

And he knows other people's suffering. The letter to the Hebrews says that "he learned obedience from what he suffered."[9] A mysterious and profound phrase. How many times do we say: *Yes, I heard that this experience was like this or that, but when I actually lived through it, I experienced it in my own flesh.* Something similar must have happened in the case of Christ. In the same letter, one verse earlier, it says, "When he was in the flesh he offered prayers

---

[8]    Is 53:3.
[9]    Heb 5:8.

and supplications with loud cries and tears." It doesn't say he prayed that way only in Gethsemane, where he sweated blood, but rather that during his earthly life he prayed to the Father with supplications and prayers, with loud cries and tears.

This text of Benedict that I recently cited really catches my attention: *"Without suffering, nothing is transformed."* The path of transformation—in the circumstances in which we live—is suffering, because we are sinners.

John Paul II, a man who knew much suffering, wrote about salvific suffering, and said:

> In his messianic activity in the midst of Israel, Christ drew increasingly closer to the world of human suffering. "He went about doing good," and his actions concerned primarily those who were suffering and seeking help. He healed the sick, consoled the afflicted, fed the hungry, freed people from deafness, from blindness, from leprosy, from the devil and from various physical disabilities, three times he restored the dead to life. He was sensitive to every human suffering, whether of the body or of the soul. And at the same time, he taught, *and at the heart of his teaching there are the eight Beatitudes*, which are addressed to people tried by various sufferings in their temporal life.[10]

He says it almost as an aside: the eight Beatitudes are in the center of the teaching of Christ, and he addressed them to those who are tried by suffering.

He goes on to say:

> These are "the poor in spirit" and "the afflicted" and "those who hunger and thirst for justice" and those who are "persecuted

---

[10]   Pope John Paul II, *Salvifici Doloris*, #16, https://w2.vatican.va/content/john-paul-ii/en/apost_letters/1984/documents/hf_jp-ii_apl_11021984_salvifici-doloris.html. The emphasis is mine.

for justice's sake," when they insult them, persecute them and speak falsely every kind of evil against them for the sake of Christ. Thus, according to Matthew; Luke mentions explicitly those "who hunger now." At any rate, Christ drew close above all to the world of human suffering through the fact of having taken this suffering upon his very self. During his public activity, he experienced not only fatigue, homelessness, misunderstanding even on the part of those closest to him, but, more than anything, he became progressively more and more isolated and encircled by hostility and the preparations for putting him to death.[11]

It's difficult to suffer hostility. I don't know if you have suffered it at some point, but it is hard, it's difficult. It's hard to understand it and hard to suffer it. At times we have to suffer a certain hostility from some person or some group of people who, with good intention, can think that it is their duty to stand up to confront and accuse you. In general, we're talking about a very benign hostility that doesn't get beyond criticism or some slight mistreatment.

In these cases, it's very challenging to reach these people; it seems that all means of approach are cut off. It's as if there were some unexplained hostility behind it, which is why it's hard to accept. I think that if it's hard to accept these small enmities, how much worse must it be to suffer a much more violent hostility, like that which Jesus Christ had to suffer from his people, from his family who considered him crazy, from the people of his time, and from the Pharisees who were the ones who should have been helping him, who should have been on his side. A hostility so great, so open, so manifest!

It's striking to me that when Jesus raises Lazarus from

---

[11]     John Paul II, *Salvifici Doloris*, #16.

the dead, the Pharisees say *we have to kill him,* instead of converting, because "if we leave him alone, all will believe in him."[12] Such great hostility that it doesn't permit them to see anything else because hatred is blind. *Anger is blind; it doesn't let you see anything good in the other. We have to be careful not to fall into that hostility.*

Some time ago, a person speaking about the politics in Argentina noted how there are some people who cultivate a certain hatred and resentment towards one politician or another. They insult the politician and cannot recognize even one single achievement of theirs. Obviously, there is a diversity of opinions about topics that are in themselves debatable, and there can be judgments made about the fittingness or morality of political action. But this type of personal hostility doesn't come from God.

Well, Jesus suffered hostility in his life, hostility against him, and Christ was aware of this. Many times he spoke to his disciples about the suffering and the death that awaited him. "Behold, we are going up to Jerusalem, and the Son of Man will be handed over to the chief priests and the scribes, and they will condemn him to death and hand him over to the Gentiles who will mock him, spit upon him, scourge him, and put him to death, but after three days he will rise."[13]

He was clear about this hostility.

Christ goes towards his Passion and death with full awareness of the mission that he has to fulfill precisely in this way. Precisely by means of this suffering he must bring it about "that man should not perish, but have eternal life." Precisely by means

12    Jn 11:48.
13    Mk 10:33ff.

of his Cross he must strike at the roots of evil, planted in the history of man and in human souls. Precisely by means of his Cross he must accomplish the work of salvation. This work, in the plan of eternal Love, has a redemptive character. . . . Christ goes toward his own suffering, aware of its saving power; he goes forward in obedience to the Father, but primarily he is united to the Father in this love with which he has loved the world and man in the world. And for this reason, Saint Paul will write of Christ: "He loved me and gave himself for me."[14]

Through his sacrifice, everything is made new.

The passage above should be re-read slowly.

Jesus goes toward his own suffering aware of its saving value. In the movie *The Passion of the Christ*, the station of the *via crucis* where Christ meets the Virgin Mary is portrayed. And in that scene, Jesus says the phrase from Revelation: "Behold, I make all things new."[15] He is aware that, through his self-offering, everything is made new. And he embraces it.

Jesus calls his disciples to do the same, to carry the cross. Many times he talks about it: "Whoever wishes to come after me must deny himself, take up his cross, and follow me";[16] "No disciple is above his teacher";[17] "If these things are done when the wood is green what will happen when it is dry?"[18] and so on. He exhorts us to carry the cross and follow along this path.

There is no other way of configuring ourselves with Christ that doesn't pass—in one way or another—through

---

[14]   John Paul II, *Salvifici Doloris*, #16.
[15]   Rv 21:5.
[16]   Mt 16:24.
[17]   Mt 10:24.
[18]   Lk 23:31.

suffering. Of course, life is not all suffering, but one aspect of it is following the crucified Jesus. At times, at the beginning of the vocational path to the priesthood or consecrated life, there is still a lot of motivation to focus on finding one's own happiness, one's own fulfillment. Alright, this is a valid initial motivation, but a lot of maturation still has to take place. No one can be a priest only because he feels fulfilled by it. There are more profound reasons. For example, Jesus didn't go to the cross to feel fulfilled. He went to the cross for another motive: his love of the Father and of humanity brought him to that sacrifice.

## The Wisdom of the Cross

It is a big step forward in your vocation when you stop worrying about self-fulfillment, about your own happiness, and about your own goals, and you are broken, you offer yourself. You are worried about others, that others know the love of Christ. It is a big step when the person realizes that he is going to persevere because there is something that has been broken inside him through the power of the Holy Spirit.

*And it is mysterious, but that's how it is: there is a power in suffering, a redeeming and purifying power.* St. Paul called it *the wisdom of the cross.* "The message of the cross is foolishness to those who are perishing, but to us who are being saved it is the power of God. For it is written: 'I will destroy the wisdom of the wise, and the learning of the learned I will set aside.'"[19] Later he continues, "For Jews demand

---

[19]    1 Cor 1:18.

signs and Greeks look for wisdom, but we proclaim Christ crucified, a stumbling block to Jews and foolishness to Greeks, but to those who are called, Jews and Greeks alike, Christ the power of God and the wisdom of God. For the foolishness of God is wiser than human wisdom, and the weakness of God is stronger than human strength."[20]

The wisdom of the cross is wiser than the wisdom of the world.

"For God so loved the world that he gave his only Son, so that everyone who believes in him might not perish but have eternal life."[21] These words pronounced by Christ in the nocturnal dialogue with Nicodemus "introduce us into the very heart of God's salvific work. They also express the very essence of Christian soteriology; that is, of the theology of salvation."[22] God saved us in this way: "God so loved the world that he gave his only Son."[23]

## The Greatest Expression of His Love

Christ wanted to save us through his own suffering, because it is through suffering that the greatest possibility of love is manifested. He says, "There is no greater love than to lay down one's life for one's friends."[24] What wisdom is in the cross of Christ! For example, when you have to forgive, as I mentioned in the beginning. *Someone has offended you,*

[20]   1 Cor 1:22–25.
[21]   Jn 3:16.
[22]   John Paul II, *Salvifici Doloris*, #14
[23]   Jn 3:16.
[24]   Jn 15:13.

*and you can't find how to forgive him: get on your knees and look at the cross of Christ—there you will find the strength.*

Or when you have to bear an illness or some suffering: get on your knees and look at the cross of Christ.

*That is to say . . .*

*How much comfort would be lacking in the world if Christ had not died on the cross!*

*How much meaning would be lacking in human suffering if Christ had not died on the cross!*

*How much more difficult would our sufferings be if we were unable to unite them to the cross of Christ!*

*How much God wanted, in his infinite wisdom, to accompany us from within during our own sufferings!*

And through the cross, he wanted to teach us the ultimate level of humility, peace, patience, purity, and hunger and thirst for justice. Contemplating the cross is like being before an open book: it always teaches us.

## The Salvation of the Cross

This has many consequences.

A major aspect of the message we proclaim is that in Christ we are saved. It is a joyous proclamation, filled with hope. But we have to remember salvation is not gained without suffering and death.

Salvation is given to us as a seed that grows in our life and takes root in a paschal dynamic—one of death and resurrection. It is especially so in those of us who are consecrated, who try to follow Christ in every way.

*It is a salvation that is simultaneously also a transformation.* We are not speaking about an exterior change but rather an *interior transformation*. And no transformation in Christ happens without blood or tears, without being broken; often something inside must be destroyed, and a kind of loss of "apparent identity" must be experienced. When we wear the suit of Jesus Christ, it is always a bit too big or small for us; it squeezes too tight here or there.

Whatever it is that we struggle with—this person that lives with me, this task that I have, this shared living situation, this class that I have to pass, this situation that I have to live, this struggle I have to understand something—all of this sets into motion the mechanisms of faith by which I rely on the cross of Christ and on my love for him to be able to face these circumstances and transform them into a sacrifice. Through this process, I look more and more like Christ.

If no one ever gave us a curt answer, or if we were to live only among people that treated us well, how would we be able to set into motion those tools given to us so that we can follow Christ? I want to clarify that I don't justify or condone anyone treating anyone else badly; what I am saying is that in life we are given opportunities for sacrifice, not just because others are sinners, but because we ourselves are sinners.

If you are accustomed to gratifying all of your desires, but you want to live as a celibate man, obviously, it will be harder for you. Not until you sacrifice yourself and accept some struggle will you achieve your purpose, by the grace of God. How can someone be transformed into a person with a pure heart without dying to oneself, without combat? What do you expect? In dying to yourself, in that combat, there is an inner breaking. How are you going to be poor in spirit if you were raised with all of life's comforts? Poverty of spirit will not happen without suffering.

How will you be patient and meek if you always want to win and be right, if you are proud? How are you going to become humbler without dying to yourself?

And this is true for each of the Beatitudes.

The Lord wants to transform you. In his book *Mere Christianity*, C. S. Lewis explains this idea when he highlights that *God wants to transform you and will do so*, but you must let him, even though you will have to suffer.

In this life *we are not called to be enlarged photocopies of ourselves*. What would we do with more of ourselves? We wouldn't get very far. *We need Christ to be in us; and that isn't going to happen without our own death so that Christ can emerge in us.*

Transformation in Christ, configuration with him, doesn't happen without suffering. Jesus said, "Whoever wishes to come after me, must deny himself, take up his cross."[25] His disciples said to him, "We want to sit at your right hand and at your left hand"[26] and *We want to be your apostles*. We priests could say to him: *We want to be your prophets in the world* or *We want to preach your Word to the multitudes.*

We always have a desire for more good things to happen: we want someday to hold twenty *Casas de la Palabra*[27] and work in fifteen high schools, and we want there to be thirty

---

[25]    Mt 16:24.

[26]    Mt 20:21.

[27]    Part of the SSJ evangelization program in Argentina for the poor from rural areas or from the slums of large cities. *Casa de la Palabra* is also part of the SSJ program for Hispanic ministry in the USA.

more vocations to our order each year. Amen. Excellent. "Can you drink the cup that I am going to drink?"[28] *Yes, yes, we can.*[29] Excellent. That is the question that he asks us.

*These are magnanimous desires,* but Jesus would say *I want you to have all these things, too, but can you drink the cup that I am going to drink?*

We will respond, *Yes, Lord, I will drink it.* And as Newman[30] says, *the Lord will accept that promise from us.*

## The Sacrifice of the Apostle

The second consequence is that one does not achieve apostolic efficacy without the suffering I have just described. *We can break through the limit of what can be achieved through our own human efforts by uniting ourselves to Christ through suffering.* It is well and good that we have programs of apostolic formation, that we strive to be efficient and are always pursuing human excellence; not only are these things good in themselves, they are very important and necessary pursuits for the apostolate. But if all of this is not "seasoned" with the sacrifice of one's own life to Christ, what is lacking is precisely that which makes our apostolate touch the hearts of others.

When there is much human excellence and things are very well prepared, people say, "Well done, this is great, how excellent!" *But when there is sacrifice, people are converted. There is an enormous difference between one and the other.*

---

[28]   Mt 20:22.
[29]   See Mt 20:20–22.
[30]   Cf. PPS, Sermon 20.

*Making it so that people want to come, making it so that people like what we offer and have a good time, that is human excellence. Achieving their conversion, that is sacrifice.* The apostle sacrifices his life. St. Paul says, "I am already being poured out like a libation, and the time of my departure is at hand. I have competed well; I have finished the race; I have kept the faith."[31] He uses a similar expression in his letter to the Philippians.[32]

Without being willing to suffer in following Christ, we cannot proclaim the kingdom, because the kingdom does itself suffer violence—as Jesus says.[33] It suffers violence within us as we fight against it in our own hearts; and it also suffers violence in society. There is an anti-kingdom.

Suffering matures us for the kingdom—or the New Situation. Benedict XVI said in the discourse I already cited:

> If there is no moral force in souls, if there is no readiness to suffer for these values, a better world is not built; indeed, on the contrary, the world deteriorates every day; selfishness dominates and destroys all. On perceiving this the question arises anew: but where does the strength come from that enables us to suffer for good too, to suffer for good that hurts me first, which has no immediate usefulness? Where are the resources, the sources? From where does the strength come to preserve these values? It can be seen that morality as such does not survive and is not effective unless it is deeply rooted in convictions that truly provide certainty and the strength to suffer for it—at the same time, they are part of love—*a love that grows in suffering and is the substance of life.* In the end, in fact, love alone enables us to live, and love is always also suffering: it matures in suffering and provides the strength

---

31    2 Tm 4:6.
32    See Phil 3:14.
33    See Mt 11:12.

to suffer for good without taking oneself into account at the actual moment.[34]

It is love that gives you the strength to suffer; you are patient in love. You are capable of assuming suffering for love of Christ, for love of others, and for love of the kingdom.

Suffering opens us to the saving action of God, making us humbler, because, as St. Paul says, "When I am weak, then I am strong." In the same passage, St. Paul confesses, "Three times I begged the Lord about this [thorn in my flesh], that it might leave me." But the Lord responds, "My grace is sufficient for you."[35]

Many times, this text is used to refer to sin, but if we read it well, we see that St. Paul is not speaking here to sin: he is referring to suffering—because he suffers anguishes, persecutions, and limits. *Three times I begged him to take away this suffering; My grace is sufficient for you, I am with you.*

Suffering helps you ask God for his help.

John Paul II says, "One can say that with the Passion of Christ, all human suffering has found itself in a new situation. . . . In the cross of Christ not only is the Redemption accomplished through suffering, *but also human suffering itself has been redeemed.*"[36]

There is no longer suffering without meaning. The same suffering has been redeemed and transformed into a path of conversion and configuration with Christ.

It is very edifying to see the great faith with which so

---

[34]   Benedict XVI, Address of July 25, 2005. The emphasis is mine.

[35]   2 Cor 12:8.

[36]   JPII, *SD* #19.

many people face the suffering that is theirs to bear, and how the faith strengthens them.

## Exercise

And so I want you to ask yourself:

1. What are your sufferings? Make a list of your sufferings. What are the things/situations that make you suffer today? Enumerate them without despising, discounting, or judging any of them.

Then, ask yourself:

2. What are the roots of those sufferings? Are there some sufferings that grow from your own fragility or sin? Do they stem from weakness or self-centeredness? From your complexes or obsessions?

   You can find those roots in your own heart, like weakness, selfishness, personal complexes, passions—some passions make us suffer obsession, anguish, envy, or loneliness. *We can offer each one of our sins as a suffering, not in its essence as sin, but rather what that sin causes us to suffer.* Tell the Lord, "It's not that I offer you my sin; I offer you the suffering it causes me—the fact that I would like to be rid of it, but don't have the strength . . . I offer it to you!"

3. Third, ask yourself if you have some suffering that comes from love, if you suffer for others, if you suffer because others don't know Christ, if you suffer for the poor, if you suffer for the people in our programs

of evangelization, if you suffer with the sufferings of others.

How many of your sufferings are narcissistic or egocentric, and how many are sufferings that come from God's providence that you can take more advantage of? The sufferings that are more egocentric can be offered with humility: *Lord, I have these sufferings, and I offer them to you.* But what you suffer for others is even more valuable because it means that you are advancing in your configuration with Christ. They are apostolic sufferings. Do you have those?

4. Next, I would like for you to ask yourself:
   How do you act in the face of suffering?
   How much suffering are you willing to accept in your life?
   What capacity do you have for seeing things in a supernatural light?
   Do you notice that you are becoming a bit more capable of suffering, that you are leaving frivolity behind?
   They say that when Don Bosco was ordained a priest, his mother told him, "Now you are a priest, John! Now you are even closer to Jesus. Remember that beginning to celebrate the Mass is the same as beginning to suffer." It is true, because the Mass is the renewal of the sacrifice of Christ on the cross. The priest says, "My body, my blood," and there, along with the Body and Blood of Christ, are his own body and his own blood. If this sacrifice isn't there, the

Mass—while still serving others—becomes for the priest an exterior ritual.

*Let's ask Christ for greater love—a love more capable of suffering. All of the martyrs and missionaries who went—and still go—to such distances to proclaim the Good News of the kingdom, where did they get their strength? Where do they get their love? Are they superhuman? No. They have asked for love and have received it; they have contemplated the cross of Christ and have been united with it.*[37]

5.  To finish this exercise, I suggest that you contemplate the cross of Christ in your room. Close the blinds and kneel on a blanket or rug so that you can stay on your knees longer and look at the cross of Christ. Really look at it. You can aid your contemplation with a text from

---

[37] Cardinal Sarah tells the story of his work with French missionaries in his native Guinea: "For three months, they camped in the forest. They lacked everything, suffering from hunger and hostility. . . . Every morning after Mass, Father Orcel, with trowel and hammer in hand, built the temporary hut that would house them. Six months later, Father Montels became seriously ill from physical exhaustion; he was called back to God on September 2, 1912, thus becoming the "foundation stone" of the mission.

Every evening, the Fathers of Ourous gathered the children near a large cross set up in the mission courtyard, as if to symbolize the heart and center of the village. We could see it form far away: we oriented our entire lives by it! It was around this cross that we received our cultural and spiritual education. There, as the sun slowly set, the missionaries introduced us to the Christian mysteries. . . . In such a setting, these men of God made great sacrifices and suffered many deprivations, without ever complaining and with unending generosity. The villagers helped them to build their huts. Then, little by little, they built a church together." Card. Sarah, *God or Nothing*, Ignatius Press, pp. 18, 25.

the Gospels, but do it without any other objective than just to contemplate the cross of Christ.

*Glory be to the Father, and to the Son, and to the Holy Spirit. As it was in the beginning, is now, and ever shall be, world without end. Amen.*

# BLESSED ARE THE MEEK: PART 2

## Knowing How to Wait

THE second aspect of meekness, or patience, is knowing how to wait. It is common to hear "Be patient" when you have to wait your turn at the doctor's office or bank.

Patience in this sense is very important because it allows you to aspire to what is great and, at the same time, be faithful in small things.

I have known many people with great desires but no patience; because of this, they weren't able to connect that great desire with today's step toward it. *The religious understanding of life is the capacity to connect the present moment with a totality of meaning.*[1] The person who is capable of connecting what he is doing right now with the totality of meaning—who he is and where he is going—that is a person with a deep religious sense.

I see patience along these lines: *a patient person, in this second aspect of meekness, is capable of connecting what is great with what is little.*

Thus it is important to work toward and ask God for a patience that becomes virtue, that takes flesh in us.

Listen, for example, to what the constitutions of the Saint

---

[1]   Cf. Luigi Giussani, *El Sentido Religioso*. Agape Libros, Buenos Aires, 2011.

John Society say about the postulant in priestly formation, how they insist on constancy, patience, and fidelity to the ordinary, "In this way, the youth will acquire strength of will through the ordinary practice of seeking one's duty," and "greatness of spirit before the changing circumstances of life, love for things done well, constancy in one's purpose, and above all, patient perseverance in the life plan laid out for him."[2] I recommend that you reflect on these points.

They go on to say, "The youth will be helped to form his character and his personal and proper style. It is important that he be able to conquer the impulses and caprices of his youthful temperament, along with getting to know himself—his virtues and defects; he must know how to correct what is excessive or lacking in respect to his treatment of and love for others."[3] Being patient is connecting what is great with what is little.

## A Human Desire in Service of the Kingdom of God

First, be patient with the exterior work of God. I think it is important that we desire great things for the Saint John Society, that we desire to see it grow; this is a human desire that is just, good, and positive, directed in service of the kingdom of God. The human desire to grow is always there; if someone owns a hardware store, he wants his products to sell, the store to grow, and to be able to open more and more stores. This human desire for growth is a positive thing.

---

[2]    Statute 72.
[3]    Statute 73.

If a person doesn't have the desire to grow, he is a bit lackadaisical. But here in the Saint John Society that human desire is a part of something much greater; it is a transformed desire, transfigured in faith, that is clearly oriented toward the growth of the kingdom—a desire that Jesus be known, loved, and served.

The SSJ is an instrument of this mission. And each of you are protagonists in the history of this society that was founded only fifteen years ago. To me, it is very important that you desire to see the SSJ grow.

I think: When will we be able to open a house in such-and-such a place? I would love to, because we know the bishop, he has invited us, we know the city; we have seen that there are many young people and universities there, a university city, and we could offer a good partnership in that environment.

When I see a great work that can be done in a place, but we still cannot work there, I feel impatience knowing that there are young people who could benefit from our work; and this is a good impatience. *But you have to be patient in order not to get discouraged;* you have to go little by little, step by step.

Discouragement goes hand-in-hand with impatience. The impatient person is consumed in the service of the moment, then gets discouraged; but the patient person is like the tortoise. Do you know the fable of the tortoise and the hare? While the hare runs and gets distracted, the tortoise goes step by step and advances slowly but surely.

## The Land That the Meek Will Inherit

It's important to want to inherit the land: "Blessed are the meek for they will inherit the land."[4] The land promised in the Bible is a gift from God to his people: "[The] land shall be your possession, a land flowing with milk and honey. I am giving it to you as your own."[5] This has eschatological resonances; clearly what God was promising was more than physical land—because in reality, the land didn't actually flow with milk and honey.

In other words, he was already promising a much greater land: the kingdom. It is the promise of a transfigured world, where Jesus's message about the New Life will be incarnate in many persons, and the kingdom will grow and advance. We will be able to live as children of the Father—as brothers and sisters—in a world much more just, fraternal, and luminous, without death or sin, injustice or suffering. *This is where we are heading, and this will take place because God will triumph.*

The meek will inherit that kingdom of God. *We will inherit it. In the meantime, we continue to work.*

Our challenge is to aspire to what is great, while being faithful in the small things; that is patience. Beware of the "theology of failure," which spiritualizes pusillanimity and condemns success.

To explain this with a sense of humor: In the theology of failure the idea is postulated—either tacitly or explicitly— that if one is a good Christian, things shouldn't go well for him; he should fail. Basically he should be faithful but not

---

[4]    Mt 5:4.
[5]    Lv 20:24.

successful, as if the two are opposed. *If you are successful, don't trust it; because if things didn't go well for Jesus, why would they go well for you?* Something like that.

*But it's not true that things didn't go well for Jesus; things did go well. Step by step, he followed his Father's plan of love. When he was lifted up on the cross, he did so freely, and in order to rise again.*

He had to face suffering, loneliness, betrayal, and the cross, but I wouldn't call that a failure. It is precisely, as we've said before, the victory of the cross. It seemed a failure at the moment; but it was really a success—unforeseen for many, but not for Christ. He had already announced that "heaven and earth will pass away, but my word will not pass away."[6]

That is why it can be a difficult balance: those who aspire to greatness could be impatient in the small things. And those who focus on small things could stop aspiring to greatness. Then it might happen that we stay with the small things and theologize them: *What is important is this person whom I am going to visit; what is important are these five children in catechesis because each soul matters as much as a million. For God, there are no numbers.*

Yes, each person has an unfathomable dignity. But at times that can justify a lack of magnanimity, a lack of apostolic zeal. It is true that each soul matters as much as a million, but it is also true that the Lord wants to save many souls!

---

6    Mt 24:35.

### By Seeking, Working, Praying . . . It Is Attainable!

That is why I insist that patience lets us connect the small things to what is great and makes us faithful to what we have to do.

When I arrived in Portland, there were eight students in the Newman Center. I admit that it discouraged me a bit. The university has twenty thousand students, and after two years of working there, there were only eight; but they were very good and motivated young people.

I said, "Lord, help me with this!" One of the deacons was working with those students, following what another priest had done, and the truth is that both of them were excellent. They had been tasked with the hardest job: breaking the ground, beginning from zero, sowing the seed, tackling the first difficulties. I arrived just in time for the first night of the Fragua Course, when forty more students came. I arrived when they were bouncing back from failure and things were beginning to improve.

Well, we worked a lot with those eight students; we put everything into them, mentoring each one, and it was a very successful plan. With that group, we organized the following Fragua Course. Twenty-three more students came and continued participating, and we helped them persevere.

We proposed a path of going deeper in the faith for those first eight students. Fr. Lucas, another of the priests of the SSJ that works in Portland, taught them a course on Theological Anthropology every week. We invested everything in those eight, and it bore fruit! By the end of the year, we had established a community of thirty students, which was an incredible growth. I hope that next year we can grow even more, maybe going from thirty to fifty! I even dare to hope for one hundred students. I won't say one thousand, but I do hope for it to be more and more successful—that it continues to generate in these young people the desire to be there, and that they feel proud to be part of the Newman Center.

I think that God wants this, and we will achieve it. I don't know if it will be this year, next year, or the following, but by seeking, working, praying, little by little and step by step, it will happen!

### Patience on Our Path to the Priesthood

Sometimes things are achieved more easily, sometimes less so. In Montevideo, we began only recently but already have a large group of university students. Of course, we still had to work for that, but it seems that the field is more fertile there. In other places, you have to work the land . . . it will happen; you just have to be patient. If you are not patient, you either downplay the situation—*with eight souls we're doing well enough*—or you begin to theologize it, or you begin to make accusations: *No, the problem is that no one lives here at the university; they all commute,* or *No, the problem is that it is a very liberal city; this is Oregon—the state with the least participation in the Church.* This may be, but what are you going to do with this diagnostic? So, you justified yourself and managed to explain sociologically why things aren't going well for you . . . And? What are you going to do? Are you going to just stop there?

The path of evangelization—especially the New

Evangelization on the frontiers of the Church[7]—requires patience. If you are not patient, you cannot grow, because things do not always happen very rapidly. *And you have to work while you wait; patience is not lying down for a nap.*

*Patience is the constant, serene, trusting, meticulous, serious, and professional work—full of faith—that in the end will bear fruit.*

That's how it was here in Pilar. I remember that five years ago we could not pull together a group of young people to persevere in a program. There seemed to be no way! They'd come to a mission trip, but then they'd leave and others would show up. We couldn't find the key to the issue.

Well, today the Fragua Program is growing, and that fills us with joy, but it didn't happen overnight. The VAE[8] also continues to grow, filling us with hope. But it took a lot of work, analysis, effort . . . and much prayer.

The other day I went to one of the slums and recalled the stories of the first ones who'd gone there—how difficult it was for them to enter the homes, the challenge of gathering the people, the desolate environment in the few meetings they were able to put together in the chapel. I wouldn't say that now we have a multitude too numerous to count, but we have a young community there that gives us hope; this is achieved with patience. When you are walking through one of these slums for the first time, you tend to say: *What am I*

---

[7]    Precisely because the New Evangelization is directed to those Catholics who are farthest away, who do not participate. It is a task of the frontier in the sense that it requires going to the known limits, beyond the group of people who come, in order to venture further, to connect with those who don't come.

[8]    Volver a Empezar: the SSJ Program in the slums in Argentina.

*going to be able to do here in this slum, with all these people
who live here? What can I possibly do?*

Newman explains that feeling when he describes Peter
arriving in Rome, lost in a hostile and indifferent multitude.[9] Without a doubt, at times you can be overcome by
discouragement when you see the number of people to
whom you want to bring the Good News!

For example, when I began to travel more, the bus termi-
nals seemed so aggressive to me. I thought: *So many people
coming and going . . . and where are they headed? How can
we evangelize this? What can we do to bring the unity of
Christ to such a varied multitude?*

Well, with patience. First, it is good to know that we are
not alone; we are only a small part of a Church that has
millions of members.

It is up to us to do our part—but with magnanimity and
patience, step by step.

And sometimes some extra patience is needed, because
some of you in this room want to become priests, but are
already adults, right? Some of you are already thirty years

---

[9]    "He saw about him nothing but tokens of a vigorous power, grown up
into a definite establishment, formed and matured in its religion, its
laws, its civil traditions, its imperial extension, through the history of
many centuries; and what was he but a poor, feeble, aged stranger, in
nothing different from the multitude of men—an Egyptian or a Chal-
dean, or perhaps a Jew, some Eastern or other—as passers-by would
guess according to their knowledge of human kind, carelessly looking
at him . . . , without the shadow of a thought that such a one was des-
tined then to commence an age of religious sovereignty, in which they
might spend their own heathen times twice over, and not see its end!"
J. H. Newman, "Prospects of the Catholic Missioner," in *Discourses to
Mixed Congregations.*

old and just beginning your path toward priesthood. Well, patience; each one has his history, his pre-history, his providential path here. Fr. Maximo was already a priest when he was twenty-eight. He had the joy of being able to say "yes" when he was still in high school; that is how God called him. Others have a different history; they were already older when they were called.

The one who is older needs more patience. I imagine he sometimes thinks: *How long am I going to be here?* Or *Oof! I still have four or five years left; this is never going to end.* As we have been saying, you have to be patient and go step by step.

And remember, our life right now already has meaning. It doesn't only have meaning when we finish our formation and are ordained priests. As we go through this process, we are doing apostolate and studying. Nevertheless, it is a more hidden life; that is undeniable. And we have a vocation for the public life, for the apostolate, for missionary action.

That is why we have to be patient, which forges character and bears fruit. It is as Jesus explained: the sower went out to sow. Little by little, night and day, every seed sown grows. We learn in that parable the patience of God and are called ourselves to exercise the patience proper to a Christian.

## The Patience of the Sower

Benedict XVI writes:

> The Lord's work had begun with great enthusiasm. The sick were visibly cured, everyone listened joyfully to the statement: "The Kingdom of God is at hand." It really seemed that the

changing of the world and the coming of the Kingdom of God would be approaching—that at last, the sorrow of the People of God would be changed into joy. People were expecting a messenger of God whom they supposed would take the helm of history in his hand. But they then saw that the sick were indeed cured, devils were expelled, the Gospel was proclaimed, but the world stayed as it was. Nothing changed. The Romans still dominated it. Life was difficult every day, despite these signs, these beautiful words. Thus, their enthusiasm was extinguished, and in the end, as we know from the sixth chapter of John, disciples also abandoned this Preacher who was preaching but did not change the world.

"What is this message? What does this Prophet of God bring?", everyone finally wondered. The Lord talks of the sower who sowed in the field of the world, and the seed seemed like his Word, like those healings, a really tiny thing in comparison with historical and political reality. Just as the seed is tiny and can be ignored, so can the Word.

Yet, he says, the future is present in the seed because the seed carries within it the bread of the future, the life of the future. *The seed appears to be almost nothing, yet the seed is the presence of the future; it is a promise already present today.* And so, with this parable, he is saying: "We are living in the period of the sowing; the Word of God seems but a word, almost nothing. But take heart, this Word carries life within it! And it bears fruit!"

I do not think that there is any system for making a rapid change. We must go on; we must go through this tunnel [of European secularization], this underpass, patiently, in the certainty that Christ is the answer and that in the end, his light will appear once more.[10]

What realistic words, but how wise and hopeful in patience!

Thus, the first answer is patience, in the certainty that the

---

10    Benedict XVI, Address to the Diocesan Clergy of Aosta, July 25, 2005.

world cannot live without God, the God of Revelation—and not just any God: we see how dangerous a cruel god, an untrue god, can be—the God who showed us his Face in Jesus Christ. It is the Face of the One who suffered for us, this loving Face of the One who transforms the world in the manner of the grain of wheat that fell into the earth. Therefore, we ourselves have this very deep certainty that Christ is the answer and that without the concrete God, the God with the Face of Christ, the world destroys itself.[11]

How true this is! *Without the cross of Christ and without his teachings, the world destroys itself.*

## Ministers of the Future of the World

Benedict XVI continues, "The first point of my response is: in all this suffering, not only should we keep our certainty that Christ really is the Face of God, but we should also deepen this certainty and the joy of knowing it and thus truly be ministers of the future of the world, of the future of every person. We should deepen this certainty in a personal relationship with the Lord."[12]

Do you like this text? It is a bit long, but it's worth it. We are ministers of the future of the world in Christ Jesus, and for that, we need patience, knowing how to wait. There are no rapid changes.

It is true that the formation for the priesthood in the SSJ is slow, but this is because *we believe that there are no rapid nor magical transformations. The New Situation is rapid in the sense that one goes from darkness to light in the very moment of conversion, but that reality is still only a seed.*

---

[11]    Ibid.
[12]    Ibid.

That seed has to take root and mature, similar to the image that the prophet Ezekiel uses of the water that leaves the temple and waters the fields, all the way to the sea.[13] The water of the New Life is like that: it has to go along inundating the fields of life, bit by bit.

*Patience is the fortitude to work not only with courage, great spirit, and magnanimity, but with fidelity to the small things:* to the study of today, to the apostolate of today, to this person who comes to see me. Really, that type of patience is not needed just during formation, but forever.

Love is always concrete. Newman speaks at length about the fact that our capacity to irradiate love is limited to a concrete number of persons;[14] "Cor ad cor"—heart to heart—whether they be one thousand, two thousand, or ten thousand persons. Patience implies this fidelity to what is concrete along with a desire for what is great.

## The Necessity of Great Desires

*The person who doesn't have great desires has selfish pretensions.* Great desires for the kingdom are cultivated in the firm determination to put Christ in the center of ourselves and, from there, go to others. But if those great desires—those holy ambitions—aren't cultivated, one runs the risk of being ambitious for oneself and one's own fame, glory, power, or comfort. If you don't desire the SSJ to grow and grow well, then you will live off of what the first of the SSJ

---

[13]    See Ez 47.

[14]    See Newman, John Henry and Katherine Tillman. *Fifteen Sermons Preached before the University of Oxford Between A.D. 1826 and 1843.* South Bend: University of Notre Dame Press, 1998.

priests—and God—were able to accomplish. You will be living off of our labor—what we achieved, the houses we opened up. You might think: *Let's see: where will I go? I will go to Cordoba; yeah, that sounds good. What will my position be? Which will be my office? Which will be my desk? What is my . . . ?*

*If you don't have great desires, you will become pretentious or find yourself thinking and saying, "Now that I am ordained a priest, what will be mine?" Instead of saying, "Send me to the frontiers" or "Where can I invest myself?" Does that sound familiar?*

It is necessary to have a great desire for growth of the mission and for vocations. After all, if you believe that we are carrying out the work of God, how could you not want it to grow?

There is a text that always moves me; it is a medieval manuscript. Perhaps you have read it at some point. It says:

A priest should be very great and at the same time small, of noble spirit as if he had royal blood yet simple as a laborer, a hero for having triumphed over himself and a man that has come to fight with God, an inexhaustible source of holiness yet a sinner whom God has forgiven. He should be lord of his own desires and servant of the weak and wavering—one who will never bend before the powerful but who nevertheless bows before the small. He must be a docile disciple of his master and leader of brave soldiers, beggar with supplicant hands and messenger who distributes from full hands, courageous through prudence and counsels, and childlike through his trust in others. He must be someone who always aspires to the heights, and lover of the most humble—made for joy and accustomed to suffering, stranger to all envy, transparent in his thoughts and sincere in his words, a friend of peace, enemy of laziness, and secure in himself.[15]

He joins the great with the small, and for that he needs ... patience. *I look back, contemplating the passing of the years, and I am surprised by the work of God. It seems both huge and little in us at the same time. And it is good that it be so.*

On the one hand, one is surprised by all the things that have happened, but on the other hand, he feels that it is little because his desire is even greater.

## Don't Let Yourself Get Irritated

The third sense of patience is the most colloquial of all: that of avoiding being irritated. An impatient person is one who is easily irritated, who gets angry. This sense is especially connected to meekness, a characteristic of Christ, who described himself as "meek and humble of heart."[16]

The exhortation to meekness is a constant in the word of God: "Put on then, as God's chosen ones, holy and beloved, heartfelt compassion, kindness, humility, gentleness, and patience, bearing with one another and forgiving one another if one has a grievance against another; as the Lord has forgiven you, so must you also do. And over all these, put on love, which is the bond of perfection."[17]

It is a very realistic text: *Bear with one another, forgive one another, have patience with each other.* If we are all sinners, what do we expect? Sometimes I feel like we don't

---

[15]    From a medieval manuscript found in Salzburg.
[16]    Mt 11:29.
[17]    Col 3:12–14.

completely believe these words. At least, it is sometimes difficult for me to believe that we constantly have to follow them. I am a little idealistic, and I tend to think, *We are consecrated—we are Christians and missionaries who have already been tested—we shouldn't have to face this friction, or these difficulties in communicating better, or this resistance to forgiving or serving with greater generosity.* But why does St. Paul say, *forgive one another, bear with one another?* Because we need it!

In Ephesians 4:2, he says, "With all humility and gentleness, with patience, bearing with one another through love." Obviously, life in common isn't merely putting up with each other: it is loving one another, getting along well, dialoging, generating joy. It should have more light than shadows.

Those who have had to live alone know this and have a higher regard for common life. The other day I was speaking with a priest who had lived alone for a year, and he told me how he valued life together even more now. When you are alone for a year, you begin to feel it. It is nice to be alone for a week, or even for two, to be able to do what one wants, but after some time passes, you don't want to keep living alone! Common life is a great thing; Jesus wanted to live with the twelve for a reason. Nevertheless, at times we have to put up with each other, right? And that is why we need to be patient.

## Self-Love

So I invite you to review the patience you have for those with whom you live—your capacity to lovingly put up with the limits of your brother. The Saint John Society is not a club where those who like each other gather; it is a society, a community that gathers those whom Jesus wants to unite. Those who are alike go to a club, but not here; no, here Jesus Christ gathers us. If it weren't Jesus who gathered us, there would be neither Christian life nor holiness.

St. Paul says, "Brothers, even if a person is caught in some transgression, you who are spiritual should correct that one with a gentle spirit."[18] He says "correct with a gentle spirit," not with acrimony, bitterness, or irritation. This instruction is also found in Romans 12:9 and following.

Self-love is the root of wrath. Wrath, like irritation, is born out of the excessive attachment of the human being to himself and to his goods, material and spiritual—his honor, place, fame, comfort, and desires.

I dare say that 90 percent of our anger, if not more, is born of self-love, whether or not we are in the right. We can be in the right, but wrath that is born of self-love brings us to say things in a harsh, aggressive, cutting way when we could do so in many other more positive and constructive ways.

Where does anger come from? The Word of God says, "Where do the wars and where do the conflicts among you come from? Is it not from your passions that make war within your members?"[19] They come from there. Maybe 10 percent of them could be holy anger, evangelical confrontation, for the glory of God and a zeal for others; that could be, as it was for Jesus Christ and also for some saints, but it is a very small percentage.

---

[18]    Gal 6:1.

[19]    Jas 4:1.

And there are also the very similar texts in the Sermon on the Mount: "You have heard that it was said to your ancestors, 'You shall not kill, and whoever kills will be liable to judgment.' But I say to you, whoever is angry with his brother will be liable to judgment, and whoever says to his brother, 'Raqa,' will be answerable to the Sanhedrin, and whoever says, 'You fool,' will be liable to fiery Gehenna."[20] The message of Jesus is clear: getting irritated, insulting, and cursing merit condemnation.

He also tells us, "Therefore, if you bring your gift to the altar, and there recall that your brother has anything against you, leave your gift there at the altar, go first and be reconciled with your brother, and then come and offer your gift."[21]

And later, "You have heard that it was said: 'An eye for an eye and a tooth for a tooth. But I say to you, offer no resistance to one who is evil. When someone strikes you on your right cheek, turn the other one to him as well."[22] How many opportunities do we have in community life for doing this, for practicing this radical teaching of Jesus; and what interior freedom it gives us!

"If anyone wants to go to law with you over your tunic, hand him your cloak as well. Should anyone press you into service for one mile, go with him for two miles. Give to the one who asks of you, and do not turn your back on the one who wants to borrow."[23] There are many opportunities to quite literally live these words, right?

---

[20] Mt 5:21ff.
[21] Mt 5:24.
[22] Mt 5:38–48.
[23] Mt 5:40–42.

The other day, I asked one of you if I could borrow a sweatshirt to go for a run. "I'll give it to you," was his response. "No, wait, I only want it just to go for a run," I answered. "If you need it, keep it." It is a joy to live in a community where the Gospel is lived each day, where there is an authentic sharing of both spiritual and material goods.

## Meekness

We could list endless ways to practice meekness, many of which are suggested in the document of SSJ customs:

- Uproot hardness.
- Uproot bitterness.
- Uproot the desire to be always right.
- Always offer a simple and heartfelt welcome.

Practicing meekness has two consequences:

- First, it perfects the one who achieves it—as with any other virtue—and second, it peacefully orders the relationship between brothers.
- The one who is lord of his interior order pours out peace all around him, because peace is the fruit of order.

The patient person, in the sense of not getting irritated—the person who has achieved that meekness that comes from love and faith—comes to have a great influence and radiates Christ. I am not speaking of pusillanimity, the attitude of one who cannot confront anything or anyone; because pusillanimity is born of fear, and that which is born of fear is destructive for oneself and others. But that which is born of love radiates much and does great good. St. Francis de Sales said that a drop of honey attracts more flies than a barrel of vinegar.

Let us remember the reward: inheriting the earth, which will come in the end but is already manifested now as peace and spiritual joy. Meekness achieves stability in God.

### Exercise

I propose that you read some examples from the chapter "Way of Life" from the constitutions, which can help us focus on growing in meekness.

- "We practice fraternal correction among us and receive with simplicity the advice from our superiors and companions."
- "We know how to forgive and ask for forgiveness, aiming to eliminate all harsh sentences from our judgment and all resentment from our hearts."

These two texts help us evaluate ourselves in our interactions and how we relate with others in each area of life together.

Spend some time praying with these two aspects of patience in mind: that of knowing how to wait and that of not getting irritated, in order to inherit the earth.

*Glory be to the Father, and to the Son, and to the Holy Spirit, as it was in the beginning, is now, and ever shall be, world without end. Amen.*

# BLESSED ARE THEY WHO MOURN

WE begin this meditation with the "Cinderella" of the Beatitudes—the one that no one ever chooses: "Blessed are they who mourn, for they will be consoled."[1] It is one of the most difficult ones to choose, because at first glance it doesn't show a virtue. Being patient, merciful, and poor in spirit, working for peace, hungering for justice . . . those are all virtues and imply a good, whereas mourning doesn't at first appear to be a virtue.

## Spiritual Mourning

It almost sounds like a contradiction: "Blessed are the unhappy." However, as with all the Beatitudes, there is first the material level to which it applies: when you are mourning, know that you will be consoled, that God isn't looking away, that he sees your affliction.

It is interesting to note that in the Old Testament there is the book of Lamentations, in which the inspired author mourns the fall of Jerusalem.

The *Catechism of the Catholic Church* says that *in Christian prayer, lamentation no longer has a place;*[2] it explains

---

[1]   Mt 5:5.

[2]   For example, in number 2630: "The New Testament contains scarcely any prayers of lamentation, so frequent in the Old Testament. In the risen Christ the Church's petition is buoyed by hope, even if we still wait in a state of expectation and must be converted anew every day.

that the lamentation of Israel is a very desperate anguish expressed before God—a kind of painful crying out before God without foreseeing any solution. Since the Resurrection, this type of prayer—this pure lamentation—has ceased to have a place because it has been replaced with Christian hope.

Of course, human beings still mourn; we often find ourselves crying out as we pass through various difficulties in life. Well then: *they will be consoled.* That is Christian hope.

## The Tears of the Apostle

We will also face this Beatitude on a second, more spiritual level, so let's reflect on those who embrace this Beatitude by their own choice.

To what does this mourning refer when it is a lamentation freely chosen?

Biblical scholars say that Matthew—inspired by the Holy Spirit—recollected the teachings of Jesus and wrote them down, above all keeping in mind those who were afflicted by the sufferings of the early Church.

St. Paul says, "We are afflicted in every way, but not constrained; perplexed, but not driven to despair; persecuted, but not abandoned; struck down, but not destroyed."[3]

---

Christian petition, what St. Paul calls 'groaning,' arises from another Depth, that of creation 'in labor pains' (Rom 8:22) and that of ourselves 'as we wait for the redemption of our bodies. For in this hope we were saved' (Rom. 8:23–4). In the end, however, 'with sighs too deep for words' the Holy Spirit 'helps us in our weakness; for we do not know how to pray as we ought, but the Spirit himself intercedes for us with sighs too deep for words' (Rom. 8:26)."

[3]    2 Cor 4:7.

And later when he enumerates the sufferings he has gone through for love of Christ, he specifically describes "toil and . . . hardship, through many sleepless nights, through hunger and thirst, through frequent fastings, through cold and exposure. And apart from these things, there is the daily pressure upon me of my anxiety for all the churches."[4] St. Paul is afflicted by the care of the churches; that is his daily preoccupation, and he considers it more difficult than fatigue, sleepless nights, hunger, and exposure.

This passage from 2 Corinthians 11 has been very consoling for me, because we all undergo sleepless nights, insomnia, preoccupation, and anguish so that things will move forward, and there are always issues that concern us about the people around us. An apostle lives through all of these situations.

The care of all the churches particularly resonates with me as I think about the care of each one of the SSJ communities, but each of us experiences this in his own measure, according to his responsibilities.

St. Paul laments, "I served the Lord with all humility and with the tears and trials that came to me because of the plots of the Jews, and I did not at all shrink from telling you what was for your benefit, or from teaching you in public or in your homes. I earnestly bore witness for both Jews and Greeks to repentance before God and to faith in our Lord Jesus. But now, compelled by the Spirit, I am going to Jerusalem. What will happen to me there I do not know, except

---

4    2 Cor 11:27–28.

that in one city after another the Holy Spirit has been warning me that imprisonment and hardships await me."[5]

*"With tears and trials,"* St. Paul says, *"I did not shrink from telling you what was for your benefit."* And we can believe that they were real tears—true tears. This isn't literary hyperbole, but rather a reality. St. Paul cries for his people, for his community, for the persons that reject the Gospel, for their problems, for the fighting that exists; he is afflicted. And he asserts, "Now, compelled by the Spirit . . ." In other words, the Holy Spirit drives him; he cannot resist; the Spirit is taking him to Jerusalem, even though he knows that tribulations and difficulties await him.

Nevertheless, notice how Paul continues, "Yet I consider life of no importance to me, if only I may finish my course and the ministry that I received from the Lord Jesus, to bear witness to the gospel of God's grace."[6] His life doesn't matter to him; he has surrendered it. Later on, he will say, "Be vigilant and remember that for three years, night and day, I unceasingly admonished each of you with tears."[7] Night and day he guided and wept for those under his care, like a mother.

In the second letter to the Corinthians he similarly testifies, "For out of much affliction and anguish of heart I wrote to you with many tears, not that you might be pained but that you might know the abundant love I have for you."[8] This is the famous letter with the tears of St. Paul. "Out of much affliction and anguish of heart, and with many tears,"

---

[5]    Acts 20:19.

[6]    Acts 20:24.

[7]    Acts 20:31.

[8]    2 Cor 2:4.

he writes, because of the problems that the Corinthians had: the divisions, excesses, competitions, doctrinal deviations, and the temptation to perpetuate pagan customs.

## Those Who Have the Sorrows of a Father

So the spiritual sense of this Beatitude points to those who are afflicted or who sorrow for others. In the apostolate, these are the people who have the sorrows of a father, who get involved and carry the weight of others' lives. *The call to the priesthood is a call to be responsible for others.*

While I was preparing this talk, I remembered a movie I saw years ago called *The Son of the Bride.* It is an Argentine movie with Ricardo Darin playing the protagonist—a forty-two-year-old restaurant owner who works like crazy but doesn't do well in his business. His mother has Alzheimer's and lives in a care facility; he is divorced, has problems with his ex-wife and her family, and has a much younger girlfriend who really loves him but doesn't understand him. He is anguished, has a heart attack, and almost dies.

There is a scene in which he wakes up in the hospital and his girlfriend is beside him asking him what he dreams of. Without thinking twice, he responds, "To go far away, to an island, to the beach—without responsibilities—to have time to read, without any kind of pressure." In other words, he wants to be "without affliction."

Now, the kind of life the protagonist of the movie longs for does keep you from some kinds of suffering, right? If you live a self-centered life, you are going to suffer less; you can surround yourself with a wall of egoism and let very few people into your life. It is clear that our lifestyle—that of a missionary priest—isn't the best one for a life with that egocentric experience.

Of course, one can choose to live that way. But in doing so, you would deprive yourself of the profound joy of loving, of being a father, of giving life, of seeing that reality can change with your contribution. In other words, you may suffer less, but you will also enjoy less, love less, and experience the sadness that egoists suffer sooner or later in life.

## Renew Your Life Choice

Thus, each of us has a choice he must constantly renew: to live for oneself or to live for others. Will you live for loving, sacrificing, and giving of yourself, or will you live to look your best in each possible situation?

As we have said, in the choice of missionary life, there isn't much room left for egoism because this life is too demanding.

Even so, there are always temptations to:

- Try to look our best always.
- Suffer as little as possible.
- Get involved as little as possible.

It is a subtle temptation, but it is there: to accommodate ourselves comfortably.

Let me suggest a prayer that can shake this: "*Lord, I want to be afflicted*; I want to embrace this." *That is, I want to worry; I want to be anguished; I want to be involved; I want to be poured out, to break, to sacrifice myself—to sow myself in others in order to give life.*

I don't want to live "in peace." Sometimes people ask

you: "Is everything chill?"[9] "No," I always respond. "Chill," no; that is not the ideal for my life. In order to live "chill," I would have chosen something else.

St. Paul even speaks of "labor pains"; to be a father is similar in ways to being a mother. *The priest is father and mother*; many times, we have to do maternal things. So I would like to ask each of you:

- Are you a father? Even if you are perhaps a little young, do you have the soul of a father?
- Are you capable of becoming involved with others and suffering for them, or are you egocentric? Being a father is not, in the first place, a biological question. It's true that biological love has strength, but that is not enough, right?

There is a Psalm that says, "Those who sow in tears will reap with cries of joy. Those who go forth weeping, carrying sacks of seed, will return with cries of joy, carrying their bundled sheaves."[10]

## Often, You Have to Sow in Tears, in the Midst of Afflictions

We have already meditated on this, but I would like you to contemplate the afflictions of Christ. For example, Jesus *mourns* for Jerusalem: "Jerusalem, Jerusalem, you who kill the prophets and stone those sent to you, how many times

---

9      "Chill" is used here as a translation for the Argentine expression: "tranqui," a shortened form of "tranquilo." It is the closest expression we have in English.

10     Ps 126:5.

I yearned to gather your children together, as a hen gathers her young under her wings, but you were unwilling!"[11]

There is a church in the Holy Land called "Dominus Flevit" that marks the place where the Lord wept over Jerusalem. It is located on the Mount of Olives, and one can observe the whole city from there. It has the shape of a tear, and in the back, there is a large window behind the altar so that while celebrating the Mass the faithful see the city that caused the tears of Jesus.

The Lord wept. He was afflicted and is afflicted from taking on the sin of the world to the point of experiencing the sorrow of death.[12]

He so cries for his friend Lazarus that the people say: "See how he loved him!"[13] He is moved by the widow who has lost her son: "When the Lord saw her, he was moved with pity for her, and said to her, 'Do not weep.'"[14] He is afflicted because Israel does not bear enough fruit, and he asks for a longer time of mercy.[15]

He sorrows for the rich young man who left, and he says, "How difficult, how difficult!"[16] He sorrows for Peter: "Simon, Simon, behold Satan has demanded to sift all of you like wheat, but I have prayed that your own faith may not fail."[17] Jesus supplicates for Peter. Supplicate is a strong

---

[11]    Mt 23:37.
[12]    See Mt 26:38.
[13]    Jn 11:35.
[14]    Lk 7:13.
[15]    See Lk 13:1–9
[16]    See Mt 19:23ff.
[17]    Lk 22:31–32.

word. It implies a certain affliction, for no one supplicates without it: we supplicate when something afflicts us. *Contemplate Christ afflicted with love for the world, for others; that is the affliction of a father who gives life to his children.* And then contrast the afflictions of Christ with our own indefinite afflictions, our sadnesses, that many times come to us as a temptation. I call these afflictions "indefinite" because they do not always have a concrete cause, nor are they born from love. Love is concrete, never abstract or generic. On this topic, Fr. Grandmaison writes:

> The passions of sadness and fear, which tend to make one pusillanimous or sullen, closed in on oneself, distrusting, discouraged or depressed, consist in all that tends to close us in on ourselves, depress us, or divide us against ourselves: false timidity, pusillanimity based in self-love; frustrated vanity that bleeds through the wound; susceptibility and jealousy; fastidiousness for the good, melancholy, disgust, servile fear of God and of the good, wallowing in the misery of life, all of that without a valid and spiritual reason. . . . To all of these phantasms, to all of these clouds, to all of this advice from smallness, from fear, from diminution and apostolic sterility, we have to say: "No. I exorcise you, spirit of sadness!"[18]

The sad passions tend to be generic: "I am sad, but I don't know why," like a species of a deep bad mood. These passions are born from self-love, from susceptibility, from false expectations, or directly from a temptation from a demon. Sadness neither comes from God nor returns to God. *God does not correct with sadness.*

For that reason, these afflictions are not blessed, and we

---

[18]    L. Grandmaison S.J., La vida interior del Apóstol, Buenos Aires, Apostolado de la oración, 1982. Translation is mine.

must reject them. We have to distinguish between apostolic affliction—a worry or an anguish about an apostolate, or something that stems from that life—from a selfish sadness that makes us enclose ourselves within ourselves. This does not come from others, but is born from ourselves, from putting ourselves in the role of victims. This must be rejected as a temptation. The monks listed it as the eighth capital sin, not because it is a sin in itself, but because it leads to sin; it leads us to false compensations: to selfishness, to evasion, to the justification of our own mediocrity.

Therefore, *this Beatitude is applied to those who mourn for others, those who become involved, who expose themselves, who spend themselves and wear themselves out.* St. Paul has an expression that reminds us of this self-giving: "I will most gladly spend and be utterly spent for your sakes."[19]

## Priestly Affliction

I would like now to make a side note: there is an apostolate in which we afflict ourselves, and that is the apostolate to those considering a religious vocation, because it is in this apostolate that our paternity most comes into play. A very strong bond of paternity is generated, so strong it makes you suffer, because the person you accompany advances and then falls back, and then advances again, and, as a priest, you are following that process with the closeness of a father. Where there is a human bond, and love, there is also suffering.

---

[19]    2 Cor 12:15.

In my experience, the vocational apostolate makes you suffer, but it is the best of all. If I go to the grave knowing that some young people continue the work of the SSJ and that they can expand the kingdom, I will be satisfied.

They say that Father Hurtado, who died when he was forty-five or forty-six years old, had sent one hundred youth to the seminary, between the diocesan seminary and the Jesuit seminary. He in his own life had presented more than one hundred priestly vocations to God! It was an enormous vocational apostolate, with an immense influence. The youth saw him and wanted to be like him, and he had a personal bond with each one.

I desire the same for each one of you in particular—not just for the SSJ as a whole—that each one of you will be an apostle of vocations.

St. Paul said, "Even if you should have countless guides to Christ, yet you do not have many fathers, for I became your father in Christ Jesus through the gospel."[20]

And with that phrase he reminds them of the deep personal bond he has with them because he wants to re-orient them in their struggles. The priestly vocation flourishes when there is a paternal bond; that is the soil *par excellence* where the call of Jesus can take root and bear fruit.

St. John Paul II said to the seminarians in Spain, "Try to give testimony to your faith and your joy. You, with your "paschal joy," are *the witnesses and promoters of priestly vocations among adolescents and youth of your age. I challenge you with all of my strength that you be the first apostles*

---

[20]    1 Cor 4:15.

*of priestly vocations.* Pray and help others so that they come to your side."[21]

And on another occasion, the Holy Father exhorted them to propose the priestly vocation to those who showed signs of having received it:

> God calls those whom he wants, through the free initiative of his love. But he also wants to call through us. That is how the Lord Jesus wants to do it. It was Andrew who brought his brother Peter to Jesus. Jesus called Philip, but Philip called Nathanael (Cf. Jn 1:33ff). You should have no fear in directly proposing to a young person, or not so young person, the calling of the Lord. It is an act of esteem and trust. It can be a moment of light and of grace.[22]

Have I been or am I—as St. John Paul II put it—a witness and promoter of priestly vocations among the youth? Am I an apostle of vocations?

## The Cry of Compunction

The second sense of this Beatitude that has been present in the Christian tradition is the cry of compunction; that is to say, weeping for one's own sin. "Blessed are those who mourn for their sin" is a well-established interpretation of this Beatitude by the Fathers of the Church.

This compunction means having a clear awareness of sin: the lack of generosity, the lack of self-giving, and the

---

[21]    Message written by Pope John Paul II to the seminarians of Valencia, Spain, November 8, 1982, https://w2.vatican.va/content/john-paul-ii/es/speeches/1982/november/documents/hf_jp-ii_spe_19821108_seminaristi-valencia.html. Translation is mine.

[22]    Message of Pope John Paul II for the XX World Day of Prayer for Vocations. Translation is mine.

lack of love. It means repenting of these and crying over them. It is a grace to be able to cry for our sin.

A key term in the Sermon on the Mount is *righteousness:* "Blessed are they who are persecuted for the sake of righteousness";[23] "Blessed are those who hunger and thirst for righteousness";[24] "I tell you, unless your righteousness surpasses that of the scribes and Pharisees, you will not enter into the kingdom of heaven";[25] "Seek first the Kingdom of God and his righteousness";[26] "Take care not to perform righteous deeds in order that people may see them."[27] Jesus is constantly returning to this term.

This Beatitude is a call to a higher righteousness: the righteous one is someone who lives as a child of the Father, in Christ Jesus, as brother to others, someone who is loyal.

*Well, we must cry because we are not righteous. We are called each day to respond with generosity, and yet we still have so much anti-kingdom in our heart, we have so much selfishness. We live as if we were alone.*

The salvation of Christ is manifested in some aspects of our life, but we also resist it in many other aspects.

If we look for an example of someone who mourns in this way, we turn to the parable of the Pharisee and the publican.[28] The publican was in the back of the church; he lamented and beat his chest, and Jesus says that he was

---

[23]   Mt 5:10.
[24]   Mt 5:6.
[25]   Mt 5:20.
[26]   Mt 6:33.
[27]   Mt 6:1.
[28]   Lk 18:9–14.

justified through this lament. Peter also cried after his betrayal and was justified.[29]

Christ is proclaiming blessed those who are aware that they live in exile, those who mourn in their souls, those who experience being far from God and the promised land, those who suffer in their flesh because they are beneath the tyranny of sin, either their own or others'. They are those who suffer because they know that Love is not loved; they feel the emptiness of things. *Love itself is not loved!* That was the cry of St. Francis.

This compunction is a gift of the Holy Spirit, as it was for St. Augustine. After much struggle and crying, he finally received the grace of conversion and was faithful to it. Crying, he gave himself to the Lord; it was a gift of the Holy Spirit. We read in the letter of the Apostle James: "Draw near to God, and he will draw near to you. Cleanse your hands, you sinners, and purify your hearts, you of two minds. Begin to lament, to mourn, to weep. Let your laughter be turned into mourning and your joy into dejection."[30] He is speaking here about this Beatitude: he asks that your joy be transformed into tears, into sadness.

*Compunction, the cry of repentance, is not desperate, but rather is filled with hope. It is consoling at the same time as it is sad because it is given, is generated, from love of God:* the sorrow for one's own ingratitude, the sorrow for bearing little fruit, the sorrow for one's own mediocrity. But at the same time, compunction is the joy of the love and the mercy of the Lord. It could not be the sorrow of the vain

---

[29]   See Lk 22:62.
[30]   Jas 4:8–9.

nor of the proud that makes us think, *It can't be I who have done this.* The blessed sorrow is the sorrow of love: *Lord, how little I have loved you, how little I have given of myself; but I receive your invitation to repent, to be converted.*

## Nostalgia for God

And there is a third sense of this Beatitude that I also want to invite you to meditate on, which is the sadness born from a nostalgia for God. It is what St. Teresa of Ávila meant when she said, "I live without living in me and the life I aspire to is so high, that I'm dying because I don't die."[31] It is the sadness of exile: "If I forget you, Jerusalem, may my right hand wither. May my tongue stick to my palate if I do not remember you, if I do not exalt Jerusalem beyond all my delights."[32]

We are pilgrims, we are going to heaven, and in the human heart there is a nostalgia that seeks God, that is not satisfied with created things. Now and then the heart feels that kind of "blessed" sadness, that is like a longing for more.

C. S. Lewis, in his book *Surprised by Joy*, describes his conversion to Christianity. And he shares the experience of a deep happiness, which he calls *joy*. He describes how even when he was not a Christian, he has those fleeting moments in which he was able to glimpse an ineffable and superior beauty, as if hidden and at the same time revealed on the

---

[31]    "*Vivo sin vivir en mí y tan alta vida espero, que muero porque no muero.*"

[32]    Ps 137:5–6.

surface of things. Reality shows its transitory character and reveals beneath it a hidden and mysterious richness.

He quickly realized that such joy could not be reduced to a mere aesthetic experience, because what is truly important was precisely what was hidden behind it, like a promise.

Like a miner, he sought these experiences of beauty, of profound happiness, but the more he sought them, the more they escaped his grasp. Finally, he saw that he was seeking the beauty of God and the nostalgia of heaven. As St. Augustine said in his famous phrase: "Lord, you have made us for yourself, and our hearts are restless until they rest in you."[33]

It is the happiness of which Jesus spoke in the Gospel: "So you also are now in anguish. But I will see you again, and your hearts will rejoice, and no one will take your joy away from you."[34]

*It is the sadness of the absence of Christ.* Now we love him, but we love in faith and we follow him in faith.

In some ways we are more connected to the riches of heaven than other persons, because we live with spiritual realities all day. And that also gives rise to this nostalgia: "Oh, living flame of love that tenderly wounds my soul in its deepest center! Since now you are not oppressive, now consummate! If it be your will, tear through the veil of this sweet encounter!"[35]

St. John of the Cross writes, "Tear through the veil": appear, draw near to me. In his Spiritual Canticle, the same saint writes, "Where have you hidden yourself and

---

[33]     St. Augustine, *Confessions,* I, 1, 1.
[34]     Jn 16:22.
[35]     St. John of the Cross, *Living Flame of Love.*

abandoned me in my groaning, Oh Beloved? You have fled like the hart, having wounded me. I ran after you, crying, but you were gone."

*I ran after you and you were gone.* There is a kind of affliction that comes from loving God; it is the desire that the human heart has for God. Yes, it can grow dull, but we who are consecrated should always keep this longing awake and burning.

A priest told me that once, as he was celebrating the Mass alone in our house on El Petrel St., in the House of Formation chapel, that he had something like a real affirmation about the mystery of the Mass: a new and more profound understanding of heart about the mystery of what was happening in that moment on the altar, of who he was and of heaven all around him. And I remember that he told me that for the rest of that day, he couldn't do anything else; he was "sweetly exhausted," with little interest in anything of this world.

Reflecting on this experience, I realized that this is why God does not give us more visions in this world, and also that the faith protects us a little: because if we were to have a clearer vision of heaven, we could not live much here on earth.

We are preparing ourselves for heaven, but the experience of it that we have here in this world is always incomplete. That is why St. Thomas no longer wanted to write anymore when he had a vision of heaven, and he died shortly thereafter. Thank God that he saw heaven at the end of his life; if he had seen it earlier, he wouldn't have written anything.

*This is all to say, there is a beauty for which we are not prepared here below. But now and then it peeks out, and when it peeks out, it leaves a sweet taste in the soul, but it also leaves a feeling of "not yet."*

### They Will Be Consoled

That is why the consolation of the presence of God is the greatest consolation that exists, and every now and then it is given to us. I think that you will experience this: the consolation of realizing that Christ is present, that he is here, that he is with you, that all of Christianity is true. And it's not that before you didn't think so, but rather that having an assent in your heart of its reality is a grace. And it brings great consolation.

That is why the Beatitude says, "Blessed are they who mourn, for they will be consoled." It is referring to these three afflictions or these three meanings:

- Apostolic afflictions,
- Compunction for one's own sin,
- Afflictions born of the longing for heaven.

Isaiah writes, "Comfort, give comfort to my people, says your God. Speak tenderly to Jerusalem and proclaim to her that her service is at an end, her guilt is expiated."[36] And Jesus promises due recompense, due consolation: "Well done, my good and faithful servant: come, share your master's joy."[37]

One minute of consolation from God is worth more

---

[36]   Is 40:1.
[37]   Mt 25:21.

than ten hours of the comfort of the world—I didn't say one hundred hours because I don't want you to think I'm exaggerating. But *one minute of consolation from God is like an echo that resounds in the soul.*

## The Joy of Consolation From God

In addition to this consolation from God, which is worth far more than any others, we also have human consolations, thanks be to God, because it is clear that we all need them.

Life has its human comforts, its human joys: the consolation of friendship, of serene prayer. The consolation of being with the poor.

The simple human joys that we experience are healthy and good; for example, I really enjoy eating oatmeal in the morning, and if there is a little fruit, it's even better. It's not that our life is suffering and more suffering.

The consolation of adventure, of things changing, of going to another country as we have in the United States, getting to know other diverse people and different cultures. These are natural human joys! And there are so many other joys that we experience as human consolations.

*The Lord is good to us.* Here's a silly example: I love getting up early in the morning, if I've slept well enough, drinking *mate* and reading the Psalms, praying the Office of Readings. I love that. It is a human consolation. I enjoy it not only because of the spirit of faith but also because I like the serenity in the morning and having time to pray. It is one way that I experience human consolation.

I love celebrating the Mass, not only because of the faith, but also because humanly I like it. I love preaching in the

Church of the Transfiguration in Argentina; now I am not often able to as I am living in Portland. But it is still a consolation and a joy, a personal pleasure, when I get the chance, as well as a human challenge to get people to respond to you. Now that joy has moved to preaching at the Mass in Portland for the university students each Sunday evening.

This is all to say that there are a ton of human joys and pleasures in this life. The consolation of seeing people draw near to God, their lives changing, and so on. Each of us could make a list of the human joys that God gives us. We need to know how to receive them and to enjoy them with a simple heart.

Isaiah writes:

> Rejoice with Jerusalem and be glad because of her, all you who love her; exult, exult with her, all you who were mourning over her! Oh, that you may suck fully of the milk of her comfort, that you may nurse with delight at her abundant breasts! For thus says the Lord: Lo, I will spread prosperity over her like a river, and the wealth of the nations like an overflowing torrent. As nurslings, you shall be carried in her arms, and fondled in her lap; as a mother comforts her son, so will I comfort you; in Jerusalem you shall find your comfort.[38]

This is lovely. "As a mother comforts her son . . ." I'm sure you experienced your mother comforting you when you were children. "So will I comfort you," the Lord promises. *"Blessed are those who mourn for they will be consoled,"* Jesus says—and that consolation begins already in this life. What then can we say about the comfort we will receive in heaven!

That is why, although this Beatitude is fulfilled in this life,

---

[38]    Is 66:10–13.

it is the one that most pulls us upward, I think. "They will be consoled" makes a clear reference to the final consolation. St. John writes:

> I also saw the holy city, a new Jerusalem, coming down out of heaven from God, prepared as a bride adorned for her husband. I heard a loud voice from the throne saying, "Behold, God's dwelling is with the human race. He will dwell with them and they will be his people and God himself will always be with them as their God. He will wipe every tear from their eyes, and there shall be no more death or mourning, wailing or pain, for the old order has passed away." The one who sat on the throne said, "Behold, I make all things new."[39]

He will wipe away every tear; they will be consoled.

And in the Letter to the Romans, we read, "I consider that the sufferings of this present time are as nothing compared with the glory to be revealed for us."[40] The afflicted, those who mourn, will be consoled.

### Exercise

I propose three meditations:

1.  In the first place, review your apostolic affliction, your capacity for commitment, and your capacity for bearing with others. Review your paternity, and also the vocational fruit that stems from it. And if God gives you the grace of tears, cry. Afflict yourself for love of others.

---

[39]   Rv 21:3–5.
[40]   Rom 8:18.

2.  Then do an examination of conscience,[41] confronting your own life with the Beatitudes. Doing so could help you make a more detailed examination of conscience.

    But before you do, put yourselves before God and ask for his forgiveness. Ask for the grace of compunction before the cross of Christ. I suggest that you do this second meditation while contemplating the cross.

    Write, and tell him, "Lord, I want to repent with all my heart."

3.  Finally, meditate on heaven and the consolation of God. Tell the Lord that you accept the sadness of nostalgia, as long as this nostalgia be a wound of love: a kind of remembrance that we are pilgrims and that our way leads us to heaven.

*Glory be to the Father, and to the Son, and to the Holy Spirit. As it was in the beginning, is now, and ever shall be, world without end. Amen.*

---

[41]    See the end of the book for an examination of conscience according to the Beatitudes.

# BLESSED ARE THEY WHO HUNGER AND THIRST FOR RIGHTEOUSNESS: PART 1

## Justice Is Holiness

WE turn now to another Beatitude: "Blessed are they who hunger and thirst for righteousness, for they will be satisfied."[1]

Here is a commentary by one of the missionaries. He writes, "The Beatitude that most resonates with me is 'Blessed are they who hunger and thirst for righteousness, for they will be satisfied.' I understand righteousness to be holiness; and by holiness I don't just mean my own, but that of the whole earth."

This is a very good summary, isn't it? Justice or righteousness in the Gospel is holiness, but this term can speak of holiness not just as something personal and individual, but as something that radiates toward others, impacting one's community and society. In this way, justice refers to a group of persons.

The commentary continues, "I see that this Beatitude touches on my personal experiences, because since my conversion, I have had a great desire to radiate it to others. What has moved me since then is the desire that every

---

[1] Mt 5:6.

person know Jesus and that little by little the Kingdom of God come into this world. I think that it is Good News for various reasons: first for what it says in the second part: *'They will be satisfied', because it renews my hope that this is not an empty desire that will never be fulfilled. I am not only speaking about heaven, but also this present life, which will be satisfied by seeing the Kingdom grow.'"*

There are two ways of saying blessed: one is subjective and the other is objective. "Blessed" is a subjective, affective state—it is what one experiences when one is content and happy, for example—but it is also an objective situation that goes beyond one's own feelings. When someone says to a teen that is complaining because he has to study, "Blessed are you who have the possibility of not only going to college but to a really good one!" There the use of the word "blessed" is not making reference to the teen being happy—in fact, he is not happy, which is why he complains—but rather that he is blessed in the objective sense. It is like telling him, "How good it is that you are going through this, how good it is in itself, even though maybe you don't realize it."

Sometimes the Beatitudes are understood in this way, objectively: "Blessed are they who hunger and thirst for righteousness," because it means that objectively they have been overtaken by Christ, and those desires present in the heart imply that Christ is already working within, through the powerful action of the Holy Spirit. Those desires are like a manifestation of his presence in the soul.

This hunger is a sign that God is alive in you, since God produces in you both the desiring and the working, as

St. Paul says.[2] And therefore that hunger and thirst, which
come from God, are an announcement of a completion, of
a satisfaction that we will achieve with our personal collaboration and with the impulse of grace. It is God who gives
us that hunger and thirst, and who gives us the means by
which the hunger and thirst can be channeled into works
for a greater justice.

## What Does It Mean to Hunger and Thirst for Righteousness?

What does it mean to hunger and thirst, and what does it
mean to hunger and thirst for righteousness? In this Beatitude, hunger and thirst are clearly a metaphor referring to
an intense desire, not to material hunger and thirst. While
Luke does refer to those who hunger,[3] Matthew clarifies
that it is a hunger and thirst for righteousness.

Jesus teaches both, which is why this Beatitude has an
application on both levels. *Blessed are those who hunger,
for they will be satisfied since God does not forget them; he
sees their suffering.* In the Gospel of Matthew, Jesus says,
"For I was hungry and you gave me food, I was thirsty and
you gave me drink."[4] Here he is referring to the material, to
the suffering of one who experiences hunger and material
needs of all kinds. God sees that suffering and will satiate it.
The prophet Isaiah had already announced this from God:

---

2    "For God is the one who, for his good purpose, works in you both to
     desire and to work" (Phil 2:13).
3    "Blessed are you who are now hungry, for you will be satisfied" (Lk
     6:21).
4    Mt 25:35.

"All who are thirsty, come to the water! You who have no money, come, receive grain and eat; Come, without money and without price, drink wine and milk."[5]

But the deepest meaning of this Beatitude, the most fundamental, is the spiritual, for Jesus is not praising a material situation, but rather a freely-chosen life of embracing the Gospel. The spiritual meaning, freely embraced, is the one that Christ emphasizes most in the context of the Gospels as a whole.[6]

That is the sense which Christ expresses in Matthew. His phrase "hunger and thirst for righteousness" clarifies which hunger and thirst the Lord means. This expression is also inspired by the Word of God when the prophet Amos says, "Yes, days are coming says the Lord God, when I will send famine upon the land: not a famine of bread, or thirst for water, but for hearing the word of the Lord. Then shall they wander from sea to sea and roam from the north to the east in search of the word of the Lord, but they shall not find it."[7]

In other words, Amos is saying, *I am going to send a hunger for the word of God, a hunger for a prophet to speak to them in the name of God, but they will not find it because of their hardness of heart.*

In Psalm 63, we find, "O God, you are my God—for you I long! For you my body yearns; my soul thirsts for you like

---

[5]   Is 51:1.

[6]   "The term 'spirit' expresses power and vital activity in the Semitic conception, the habitual interior dispositions that orient a person's acts. It is an attitude toward life itself." Francisco Bartolome Gonzalez, *Acercamiento a Jesus de Nazaret 2.* Madrid:Ed. Paulinas, 1985, 6–19. Translation is mine.

[7]   Am 8:11–12.

a land parched, lifeless, and without water."[8] Again we see the Word speaking of thirst for God.

Then in the desert, before the Sermon on the Mount, Jesus responds to one of Satan's temptations: "One does not live by bread alone, but by every word that comes forth from the mouth of God."[9] This constant link between material hunger and spiritual hunger is a fully biblical metaphor.

*It's clear, then, that hunger and thirst refer to a deep-seated and urgent desire.*

Have any of you ever been thirsty? Really, terribly thirsty? It happened to me once, on my high school graduation trip. We climbed a mountain, hiking upward some four or more hours without water, thinking that there would be water along the way, but there wasn't any. We had to hike four hours back down again, and I experienced the worst thirst I've had in my life. It was a desperate thirst! We ran down the mountain not even caring if we twisted an ankle or fell, the thirst was so terrible. I believe thirst is worse than hunger, for it is a most primal need.

That is why this metaphor of hunger and thirst is so powerful. What is the hunger and thirst for? For righteousness. And not just any righteousness, since in the Bible righteousness is holiness. It's a thirst for the righteousness Jesus speaks about in the Sermon on the Mount: a righteousness that is superior to the law of the scribes and Pharisees.

The righteous are those who seek the will of the Father, as Jesus says, "Not everyone who says to me, 'Lord, Lord,'

---

8    Ps 63:1.
9    Mt 4:4.

will enter the kingdom of heaven, *but only the one who does the will of my Father in heaven.*"[10]

For Matthew, righteousness is the desire to live like Jesus in a new society, in the New Situation, in which the law is Jesus himself. The new society of Jesus's brothers and sisters—those who do the will of the Father—brings about that righteousness that Jesus summed up in the commandment to love one's neighbor.

In other words, we experience righteousness in the measure in which the New Situation takes root within us, to the extent that we live in Christ as children of the Father, with others as our brothers and sisters.

While it begins as something personal, it goes on to impact society; *for as more of us begin to live it, the kingdom becomes visible.*

Hence making this Beatitude merely about social justice would diminish it. A social justice is indeed implied, since the kingdom of heaven is made visible and touches all of society, but the kingdom is not reduced to the social. Salvation must not be equated with liberation from social oppression, which is a fundamentally political task. But if this political task is carried forward by competent Christians, who by nature of being Christian have a special sensitivity for the poorest and act because of it, then it becomes apparent that the justice or righteousness of the Sermon on the Mount is also capable of integrally permeating political action and social structures.

---

[10]   Mt 7:21ff.

## The Danger of Losing the Vertical
## Dimension in Consecrated Life

A few years ago, I met a North American missionary organization. At the American Missionary Congress in Paraná, Argentina, I had the opportunity to meet with their superior general, who was an upright man with a great love for the poor.

He had lived in various countries in Latin America and had been a missionary for many years before moving to Chicago and New York, where their centers of formation are located. The organization had begun as a Society of Apostolic Life dedicated to the mission *ad gentes*, to those who don't yet know Christ. It received priests and seminarians who wanted to mission, and it organized, formed, and sent them.

Endorsed by the North American Conference of Bishops, it used that authority to form and send priests to mission countries—first to China, then to other countries in Asia. It is now in Asia, Africa, and some Latin American countries.

All of the priests were North Americans, but their idea was that these American priests would go as missionaries to other places and foster local vocations. It had been a flourishing and, in the best sense, a powerful organization: full of vocations, good works, and evangelization. But now it appeared to be dying.

These men were excellent people, all older, selflessly-giving priests, but they exclusively centered on social action. In practice, they had equated Christ's mission to works of social action—all very important, of course—like installing a clinic, building access to water, etc.

In their contact with the poorest people in Latin America, they were strongly influenced by a certain theology that, in practice, equated salvation with social liberation, and they transmitted that theology to their whole organization. Now they have neither vocations nor momentum. Why?

Among other reasons, it is because young people are not interested in giving their life to an organization almost exclusively dedicated to social action. What is tragic is that it had begun with a strong evangelizing mission to clearly announce the Good News and it ended up as a North American non-profit organization run by people of faith. In the process, it lost all of its enchantment, all of the personality and focus proper to consecrated life.

All of the priests I met seemed to me to be upright and honest men with bold convictions, but they had lost what is often called the "vertical dimension" of consecrated life: being rooted deeply in God, not just doing his work. They had lost the certainty of the New Situation of Christ. And when an organization loses that certainty, it runs the risk of transforming into a merely philanthropic agency.

## Life in Christ, the Transforming Factor

This story illustrates how the hunger and thirst for righteousness, which come from on high and constitute a grace deeply rooted in the heart of Christ, suffer the temptation of being transformed into a mere search for greater social justice.

We know that, to a generous heart, others' needs are

obvious and the desire to help is spontaneous, *but we have to sustain the vertical dimension of life and put God first.* This means comprehending and accepting that the justice of which Jesus speaks is, first and foremost, holiness. In some ways, life in Christ is more visible than social progress, right? It is visible in its fruit, but spiritual in its root.

*We have this spiritual focus that we must protect,* and that is why we don't want to rely on our own works, because relying too much on our own works, with time, tends to weaken that focus. The spiritual dimension is weakened if you only dedicate yourself to social action. One runs the same risk by dedicating oneself, for example, to running a school. Over time you can forget the reason for that school, which was for evangelizing, right? Then it becomes an end in itself, as happens to so many institutions. It happens with some Catholic schools, which have many young and excellent people, and it is painful to see an opportunity lost because there is no serious work of evangelization. How could this happen? They are academically excellent and prestigious, but if they do not evangelize, they lose the fundamental character that makes them Catholic.

Here in the USA there are many prestigious Catholic universities that have aligned themselves with the world by the message they proclaim through their teaching faculty. They have lost the specific character and contrast to the world that a Catholic university could offer and have instead conformed to the world's standards.

*We, by the grace of God, have the certainty of the New Life* and an understanding of its relevance. We are blessed because we do hunger and thirst for justice in the way that Jesus Christ understands it—as a desire for holiness.

Therefore, our hunger and thirst for justice are primarily vertical because they come to us from God; only in this way will they have a transforming impact on society.

*On the positive side, we believe that persons who live in Christ transform society and the world.* The flip side is that the world cannot be deeply transformed except through life in Christ.

Jesus said, "Without me, you can do nothing."[11] That is why we have this hunger and thirst for righteousness, for justice, for becoming saints, and for helping others to become saints. We seek to sanctify ourselves through sanctifying others, with the deeply rooted conviction that holiness lived through the vocation of each person is what deeply transforms the world.

Jesus said in the Sermon on the Mount, "Seek first the Kingdom of God and his righteousness, and all these things will be given you besides."[12] They will be given to you. In other words, when we preach the kingdom, the rest will arrive as fruit, as a result of the growing kingdom. For that reason, we seek to dedicate ourselves with all of our energy to evangelization, and we believe that in dedicating ourselves to this, we are close to the heart of the Church.[13]

---

[11]  Jn 15:5.

[12]  Mt 6:33.

[13]  "The Church knows this. She has a vivid awareness of the fact that the Savior's words: 'I must proclaim the Good News of the kingdom of God,' apply in all truth to herself. She willingly adds with St. Paul: 'Not that I boast of preaching the Gospel, since it is a duty that has been laid upon me; I should be punished if I did not preach it.' It is with joy and consolation that at the end of the great Assembly of 1974 we heard these illuminating words: 'We wish to confirm once more that

The Saint John Society contributes to the world's transformation with the New Evangelization, because in this way it brings into history *the most powerful transforming factor*: New Life in Christ.

We call, form, and send lay people to the world so that they can be salt and light.[14] The call is proper to the mission: it is our effort to reach those who are farthest away with an offer that enables them to encounter Christ in the midst of a community.

Formation begins when the person has accepted Christ as his Master and embarks on a gradual and progressive path of growth in Christian life—a path that includes the human, spiritual, doctrinal, and apostolic dimensions. Upon completing the formation, he is "sent" so that he can bear fruit and serve in the Church and in the world. It was in the same way—little by little and from within—that Christians transformed the ancient world almost without trying, and we are called to continue doing the same today.

---

the task of evangelizing all people constitutes the essential mission of the Church.' It is a task and a mission which the vast and profound changes of present-day society make all the more urgent. Evangelizing is in fact the grace and vocation proper to the Church, her deepest identity. She exists in order to evangelize, that is to say, in order to preach and to teach, to be the channel of the gift of grace, to reconcile sinners with God, and to perpetuate Christ's sacrifice in the Mass, which is the memorial of his death and glorious resurrection." Evangelii Nuntiandi, Pope Paul VI. (http://w2.vatican.va/content/paul-vi/en/apost_exhortations/documents/hf_p-vi_exh_19751208_evangelii-nuntiandi.html).

[14] See Mt 5:13.

## Love of God

Let's focus now on our prayer life, which nourishes the vertical dimension of life: empowering, forming, and protecting it.

Organizations that lose the vertical dimension quickly lose their life of prayer. Masses become mere popular celebrations; personal prayer is reduced to the minimum. That is why we insist on the care of the chapel—the neatness of the altar cloths, the candles, the cleanliness. These things protect the vertical dimension, fostering and expressing it. And that is why for Sunday Masses we focus so much on celebrating with piety, insisting that there be music that encourages prayer and lighting that fosters spiritual recollection. In other words, we are trying to make it so that the mystery of the Mass, though unfathomable, is relevant for those who attend. We want to build a bridge between the objectivity of what is truly happening there on the altar and the subjectivity of those perceiving it, that they may grow in faith. Each Mass has enormous evangelizing potential.

Fr. Cantalamessa writes, "The first and most essential proclamation that the Church is charged to take to the world, and that the world awaits from the Church, is that of the love of God. However, for the evangelizers to be able to transmit this certainty, it is necessary that they themselves be profoundly permeated by it—that it be the light of their life."[15] Being intimately permeated by this certainty of God's love means that *the love of God is the light of your life.* This is something we must nourish constantly.

---

[15]   Raniero Cantalamessa, Second Lenten Homily, April 1, 2011. (https://zenit.org/articles/father-cantalamessa-s-2nd-lenten-homily/).

## Vocation; Hunger and Thirst for Prayer

Prayer is very important. It isn't one more task or one more item to check off your to-do list—you meditated on the Gospel, you visited the Blessed Sacrament, you prayed the Rosary, etc. That's how it is in the beginning, which is good, because you are struggling to fulfill duties and incorporate habits. But prayer is so much more than that! It is a need for those of us who are consecrated; a hunger and thirst for righteousness in the evangelical sense is expressed in a hunger and thirst for prayer. A person with a vocation hungers and thirsts for prayer, desiring not only to pray, but to pray more.

Prayer expresses our need for intimacy with God—for tenderness, friendship, and closeness. It is dialogue with Christ, and with the Father in Christ, through the Holy Spirit. Through prayer, we inhabit the Trinity and the Trinity inhabits us. And we begin to live, little by little, in the continual loving presence of God. How beautiful it is to live like this!

"Whoever loves me will keep my word; my Father will love him, and we will come and make our dwelling with him,"[16] Jesus says.

*Through prayer, we are introduced to the heart of Christ.* The constitutions of the SSJ say, "Jesus, in dialogue with the Father, is the Master of our prayer. He teaches us, as he taught the apostles, to listen to the Father and to respond to him. We live our prayer as a grace of participation in the prayer of Christ. It springs from Christ as if from a fountain and goes to the Father by means of him, with the

---

[16]    Jn 14:23.

Spirit of Christ that 'intercedes for us with inexpressible groanings.'"[17]

Our prayer is first of all a grace, a gift from God. Through that grace, we participate in the prayer of Christ; we enter into the heart of Christ, and in him, we pray to the Father.

Our prayer springs forth from Christ—in each one of us—like a fountain that goes toward the Father through Jesus, with the Holy Spirit interceding for us with inexpressible groanings. He gives us his feelings, causes us to praise him, prompts us to offer ourselves up, brings us to the Father.

As we go to the Father, we bring along all the people for whom we intercede and all the situations we wish to present to him, and so we begin to enter into the prayer of Christ. And, let me tell you—you who desire to be a priest—when you celebrate the Mass, that is the prayer of Christ *par excellence*. It is the offering of Christ to the Father that recapitulates your whole day, including all that you have lived and all the people who have had contact with you. All are gathered there, in the Mass. There the prayer of Christ to the Father is gathered up, as well as our prayer to Christ—the Friend with whom we share life—and always accompanying it, our prayer to the Blessed Virgin.

### Illuminative Life

"We aspire to an illuminative development of the spiritual life, a positive following of the Lord that creates new

---

17    Rom 8:26.

persons. It is not enough to repeat devotions; it is about experiencing life in Christ through the power of the Spirit."[18]
What is the illuminative life?

Fr. Tanquerey's book helps to answer this. Following a more classic model, he divides the spiritual life into three stages: the purgative life, the illuminative life, and the unitive life. He says, "Once the soul is purified from past faults by a long and arduous penance, in keeping with the number and gravity of those faults, and once it has been grounded in virtue through the practice of mortification and resistance to disordered inclinations and temptations, then it enters into the illuminative way. This stage of the spiritual life is thus named because the great aim of the soul is now the imitation, or Following of Christ, by the positive exercise of the Christian virtues. Jesus is the Light of the World, and whoever follows Him does not walk in darkness."[19]

It is during the illuminative stage that one begins to make gains in the struggle against sin—at least the most serious sin—and focuses on configuration with Christ.

He continues, "St. Teresa thus describes the inhabitants of the third mansion—in other words, the souls that are more advanced in the spiritual life: 'They have an intense desire to not offend the Divine Majesty: they avoid even venial sins; they love penitence; they spend hours in recollection; they employ their time usefully; they perform works of charity toward their neighbor. Everything about

---

[18]    Statutes ASJA, #16 – The constitution of the Association of Saint John Apostle, the lay group associated with the SSJ.

[19]    Adolphe Tanquerey, *The Spiritual Life: A Treatise on Ascetical and Mystical Theology Second and Revised Edition,* trans. Herman Branderis, Brattleboro: Echo Point Books, 2015, 961.

them is in perfect order: their words, their clothes, their homes.'"[20]

Pay close attention to the following text, where he describes some signs of those who are entering into the illuminative way:

> We make Him the center of our thoughts. We love to study His life and His mysteries. The Gospel presents to us new charms: we read it slowly and affectionately; the least details of Our Savior's life, especially His virtues, hold a deep interest for us. We find in the Gospel an inexhaustible source of subjects for our meditation. We love to ponder over the words of our Lord, to analyze them and to apply them to ourselves. When we wish to practice some virtue, it is in Jesus that we study it first of all, recalling His teachings and example and finding there great motives for reproducing in ourselves His own dispositions and virtues. It is on Him that we focus our thoughts during Holy Mass and Holy Communion: the liturgical prayers become for us an excellent means of studying Our Savior. Lastly, by devout readings we strive to gain a deeper knowledge of His doctrines, especially of His spiritual teachings. It is Jesus we seek in books.[21]

## The Presence of Christ in Our Lives

Christ becomes the center of our hearts and our thoughts; in him, we begin to live in the continuous and loving presence of the Father. Now, that does not prevent us from doing all that we have to do. On the contrary, we encounter the presence of Christ in our daily life.

Tanquerey continues:

> Love leads to *imitation*. The very fact that we prize the qualities

---

[20]    Tanquerey, *The Spiritual Life*, 962.
[21]    Tanquerey, *The Spiritual Life*, 966.

of a friend and are drawn to him by those qualities causes a desire to reproduce them in ourselves, so as to be one with him in heart and soul; *for we feel that our union will not be strong and deep unless we share in the thoughts and feelings and actions of our friend.* We instinctively imitate the one whom we love. And thus it is that Jesus becomes *the center of our actions*, of our whole existence. When we *pray*, we draw unto ourselves Our Lord with His religious spirit, to glorify the Father and effectively beg for the graces that we need. When we *labor*, we unite ourselves to the Divine Artisan of Nazareth, to work as He did for the glory of God and the salvation of souls. When we want to *acquire some virtue*, we draw to ourselves the perfect model of that virtue, Jesus; and with Him we strive to practice it. Even our *recreation* is taken in union with Him and in His spirit, with a plan to labor later on for the great interests of God and His Church.[22]

When I read this, the part about recreation catches my attention, because when I was in the seminary and first ordained a priest, I liked to go running while listening to secular music—a certain kind of music with a good beat. One day I decided: "Enough of this already!" It was difficult for me to run with Christ while listening to that type of worldly music because I was running disconnected from Christ, as if inside a parenthesis or a bubble. That is why I decided to run while listening to Christian music with a good beat. There are steps that one takes when desiring a greater presence of God.

---

22    Tanquerey, *The Spiritual Life*, 968.

# BLESSED ARE THEY WHO HUNGER AND THIRST FOR RIGHTEOUSNESS: PART 2

O NE of you once told me that he experienced some resistance to analyzing his own prayer. He said, "I'd rather analyze Christ than myself." That is fine, but sometimes one has to analyze oneself, even if it makes prayer less affective. I recommend that you go back and contemplate Christ praying in many of the Gospel passages. See how Christ prays and lives in that mystery of communion with his Father.

Inspired by him, perhaps we can rethink and review this Beatitude of "hunger and thirst for holiness," which is manifested not only in a hunger and thirst for spiritual life and growth in love for Christ but also in exploring our interior landscape, advancing in prayer rather than staying content with repeated devotions, and growing deeper in the illuminative and unitive life, as the saints did.

## Called to Holiness

They say that St. Philip Neri was found with an enlarged heart because of how much love he had for Christ; St. Francis of Assisi was so configured with Christ that, at the end of his life, he received the stigmata. While we do not seek these extraordinary things, what we can and are called to seek is holiness: our own, personal, dynamic holiness in the context and situation of the Saint John Society. *The Lord calls us to grow, not to remain static.*

Some years ago, each of the priests received a gift: a photo of an old man, hunched over and kneeling, praying a rosary. He was a priest. I love that image because it makes me want to be old in the same way as that ancient priest on his knees, piously praying the Rosary.

We need that hunger and thirst for internal growth. We also want a hunger and thirst for others to grow in holiness. We have already meditated on this idea, but I would like to return to it within the frame of this Beatitude. *The desire of Jesus's heart is that the Good News of the kingdom spread; therefore, it is important to hunger and thirst for the righteousness of others.*

St. John Bosco said, *"Da mihi animas caetera tolle,"* which means, *Lord, give me souls; keep the rest, take the rest from me.* The thirst for souls—that others also live in Christ and experience the New Situation—is awakened by the contemplation of the world around us. You might see two people from the same family, one of them living in Christ while the other does not, and you can see how different those lives are from each other. That observation leads you to desire a greater holiness for others, to have an apostolic desire.

That desire is a gift of your vocation and comes from on high, but it is also rooted in what is natural. It's easiest if we naturally have this hunger and thirst, but if not, then you must foster it!

## Human Hunger

In Villa Dolores there was a man called "El Chipá." He was a convert who had been a boxer and a boxing trainer, and he had done the Cursillo retreats. One day we were speaking about another boxer, and he said to me, "Yes, he's good. He has good technique, but he lacks hunger; the best boxers get into the ring hungry." He was not speaking about material hunger, but about the hunger for glory, the hunger to win. In that moment, I thought, *It's true: you have to have a bit of this hunger in life.* It's natural; some people have more hunger than others, more ambition and desire for glory, for triumph and success, for doing something worthwhile.

When that human hunger is touched by grace, and those two hungers combine, the former is transformed. *The egoism and narcissism are taken out of it, and it's placed in the service of the kingdom. It is a mighty transformation because a new power surges forth that channels the hunger toward the good.*

These two hungers that meet—one comes from below, the other from above—are mutually empowered.

Maybe you are not a person with a lot of hunger; perhaps you are more easygoing, without much ambition. If that is your case, *well, Lord, help me.* Grace can touch nature: *Help me to have more human hunger to achieve and let me grow in hunger for your kingdom; let those two hungers come together.*

The fact is, we need both of them. If you are going to take an exam, ideally you want to do well. That hunger for getting a good grade is a positive thing. Would you ever want to do poorly? Impossible. Later the moment for rectifying that human desire will come, for offering it and even breaking it, because you'll have to take a step of surrender. But, in principle, that hunger is something good.

So I ask you: Are you a person who hungers and thirsts? Do you have ambitions? Do you have desires? What are they? How do you perceive yourself? And your human desires and hunger, have they encountered in you the hunger of Christ—the hunger for the kingdom?

## Great Desires

Jesus said, "To the other towns also I must proclaim the good news of the kingdom of God, because for this purpose I have been sent."[1] We also know that he "was preaching in the synagogues of Judea."[2] This attitude of Christ reveals a great hunger and thirst for the growth and advancement of the kingdom.

We are talking about an intense desire. The one who hungers possesses a certain liveliness; the one who does not hunger is a bit dull, as if asleep. When a person is dull like this, not very savvy, sometimes it is because he lacks hunger.

In the apostolate, we often see this. The one who hungers to bring others to Christ is alert and does not miss an opportunity; as soon as he can, he generates an encounter, initiates a conversation, loans a book, extends an invitation. He creates space and makes things happen. For the one who does not hunger, there is always some unresolved difficulty. *Oh, he didn't have his phone. Oh, my computer broke, so I couldn't send that email. Oh, two weeks have gone by; yes, yes, the person told me that they would like to*

[1]     Lk 4:43.
[2]     Lk 4:44.

*encounter God, but . . . right then we had to . . .* It's as if the one who does not hunger is always half asleep!

In the apostolic life, a bit of that hunger is necessary, isn't it? Of course, it must be a human hunger that has been touched by grace; otherwise, it is not worth much. I could give a thousand examples, but I'll leave you with this one: In any encounter, the one who hungers for the kingdom of God immediately notices what's around him, watches, and observes to see who might be open to dialogue . . . and he draws near.

Fr. Sebastian relates that when he was traveling from Italy to Croatia, he was alone in the covered area of the boat and began to pray: *Lord, show me who you want me to do apostolate with on this trip.* Not long after that he saw an Italian family from Milan, who were headed to the beach. They were far, far away from the Church. Yet they began to converse with Fr. Sebastian about the Virgin and Medjugorje.[3] As a result, this family took a day of their vacation to go to Medjugorje. They spent the whole day with Fr. Sebastian, went to confession, and returned to God. Some time later, this family invited Fr. Sebastian to come to Milan to preach a retreat for a group they had called together. These were their friends who had also been far from God. You see? That is hunger and thirst for righteousness!

When you begin an apostolate, there is obviously the challenge of the conquest: you need to begin well in order for others to accept you and establish bonds with you. Of course, this is not really about you, it's about leading others to God, and any desire to be in the center needs to be

---

[3]   A place where Our Lady is said to appear.

purified. But you need this hunger because without it, the people you want to reach cannot come to believe in the Lord. If I am the bridge for others to believe in God and those people detest me, it will be difficult for them to love Christ. That art of conquest, of challenge, requires this kind of hunger. I must ask myself: *What am I going to do in order to draw near to this person in order to draw them to Christ?* It calls for reflection, observation; you must find your bearings in the situation.

Why am I telling you this? *Because when something interests you, when you hunger for something, you seek it out. At times you meet someone in the apostolate who generally seems half asleep, but then all of a sudden something interests him and he snaps out of it.* For example, perhaps a family member comes to visit him and, because he wants everything to go well, he arranges everything down to the last detail, and the event goes perfectly. It then becomes clear that he's not always half asleep, but rather he lacks that hunger for the things of the kingdom. Does that make sense?

That's why when things don't go well for us, we have to ask ourselves: is it because this doesn't interest us very much? *When we aren't very interested in certain things, we don't make use of all the means within our reach; we don't examine ourselves much, we don't get very involved, we always find excuses. In the end, we just don't have a hunger for them.*

## Called to Give Everything

We are called to hunger and thirst for others' holiness. It is a hunger for the kingdom, for the New Situation, for evangelization. We must desire that each program advance, that many people attend, that this retreat be a success, that in this conference the Holy Spirit give abundant fruit, that this brochure has the power to attract, that the songbooks are out and the guitar is tuned, and so on. We desire that everything run smoothly and that people be invited on time, that the talks be properly spaced and the team fully motivated. You need quite a bit of hunger for all of that.

As we have already discussed, we must have hunger and thirst for the society to grow, as well as a hunger for communicating and transmitting that hunger to others. We wish to awaken a fire in other people.

Furthermore, we hunger for a more effective evangelization of the poor. We hunger to better comprehend what we have to do—for example, in the Córdoba prison—so that the apostolate be blessed. Right now the priests in Córdoba go to the prison every week, and it is a great challenge. They are still assessing what is needed there. Instead of sitting back and saying, *Well, let's just go . . . that's good enough,* instead they hunger to do more, to reach farther, higher, deeper. *The one who hungers seeks, tries, fails, goes back and tries again, leaving all excuses behind in order to keep the hunger alive.*

I don't think you can be a priest in the SSJ if you don't experience that hunger. How could you be a missionary without it? That hunger is a sign of having discovered a mission that is part of your deepest identity.

I remember before my ordination I made a retreat in the Abba Padre Monastery in Los Cocos. I took a little time to reflect on my life, and though the thought had occurred to me before, I realized with greater clarity how everything that had happened in my entire life had prepared and brought me to the moment of my priestly ordination.

I could see clearly how, in God's providence, things "conspired" to bring about my vocation: disconnected events in my childhood and adolescence, which once had seemed to be without much meaning. Everything, absolutely everything, had conspired for the good and made sense in light of that crucial point of my life: my priestly ordination.

I think that is a sign that a person has found his place: when he comes to see how what he is doing expresses who he is. *God thought me into being to do what I'm doing now. I was born for this.* We don't often have that certainty in the beginning, but it grows with time.

That is the reason *this mission awakens my hunger: because it has managed to set into motion all that is best in me.*

Can you see this in yourself? All the resources God has given you throughout your life—your education, your family, the good things you celebrated, the sorrows you suffered, what you learned, the good and the bad—are like an army that, when the clarion call of this mission resounds, stands up and comes into play. We have soldiers anxious to fight this battle. We work to put all our resources toward the service of this mission because "for this I was born, for this I have been sent,"[4] as we can say along with Jesus.

When a person is capable of seeing what I have just described, he ardently desires to put all of his resources into the service of this mission, which he finally realizes is the one God gave him. And hunger is awakened. He is no longer goofing off, but playing the most important game of his life.

---

[4]     Jn 18:37.

Why, for example, Martin, did you attend that high school where we worked? So that you could be in the Saint John Society. If you hadn't gone there, you wouldn't be here now. God allowed you to be in that place, in that moment and . . . it was *for this*. It is not something that happened by chance. *At times you can get a bit dizzy thinking: If I had gone to another high school, or if I hadn't gone on that retreat, or if I hadn't met that person that afternoon who invited me . . . I would not be a priest today.*[5]

That's how it is: it is a mystery of the providence of God, who has been preparing me for this through mysterious paths. And I can see them when I look back.

In one of his sermons, Cardinal Newman describes how it is easier to discover the providence of God in our life if we look back on our history. Then we discover with wonder God's loving design for each one of us. He says:

> Such is God's rule in Scripture, to dispense His blessings silently and secretly, so that we do not discern them at the time,

---

[5]   Fr. Lucas very accurately describes the process of the vocational path: "The vocation is not an indefinite a priori aspiration, already located in the person; it is rather a grace that is awakened and grows *thanks to the encounter with concrete persons,* to the interaction with others who have similar aspirations, to the motivation that living examples can give, to prayer and shared apostolate. The vocation is the fruit of the encounter of an interior aspiration that comes from on high with the *providential signs* which are given in the Church and in history. These act as *events that interrupt the liberty of the person, question the person, and motivate him or her to a radical surrender for the Kingdom of Heaven.* In these signs the candidate recognizes the possibility *of realizing his deepest aspirations,* as if he were to have been born for it. The fact of being acted upon from outside, nevertheless, proves to be more in keeping with the nature of the Christian vocation, in which God always takes the initiative." Ratio Studiorum of the SSJ.

except only by faith, afterwards. . . . And so, again, in a number of other occurrences—not striking, not grievous, not pleasant, but ordinary—we are able afterwards to discern that He has been with us, and like Moses, we worship Him. Let a person who trusts he is acceptably serving God as a whole look back upon his past life, and he will find how critical were moments and acts that at the time seemed the most indifferent: like, for instance, the school he was sent to as a child, the occasion of his meeting with those persons who have most benefited him, the accidents which determined his calling or prospects, whatever they were. God's hand is ever over his own, and He leads them forward by a way of which they know not.[6]

## Exercise

1.  Do you hunger and thirst to grow in the spiritual life? To love the Lord more?

2.  The idea of growth . . . does it attract you?

    Because frankly—and here I speak to you, young men with a priestly vocation—in your life there will be adventure, as there is in my life and in the life of every dedicated Christian. But you will be ordained priests, God willing, and will go to other places where you will have to begin, create, generate, become founders. There will be work with youth, adults, and programs, where you will meet some people today and others tomorrow. You will work with the poorest of the poor and with those in prison. There will always be new doors to open and new bridges to build.

---

[6]   John Henry Newman, "Christ Manifested in Memory." PPS IV, 17, 253–266.

But let it be clear that this priestly missionary life *is not sustainable if there is not interior growth in love—because it will become boring, like any life.* Even change itself can be boring. I don't know what life might seem the least boring to you, but let's suppose it's a life as a ski instructor in Andorra. How exciting! Well perhaps, until the fifth ski season when you realize it's always the same. Even those who go from place to place as vagabonds get bored of that. *The only thing that saves you from boredom is love.*

*We cannot deny having a longing.* Here in the SSJ the perspective of interior growth is very important, because for us, it is our greatest longing. Everyone has a longing for something. Either I desire worldly success, to be a cardinal for instance, or I desire to grow from within. Either I desire to have power, or I desire to love the Lord more. But I always have some desire, some longing within me.

What is your longing? To what does it attract you? Where do your desires lead?

*Hunger and thirst are graces that come with the vocation,* as is growing in the desire to love. I have the desire to grow in love. Sometimes I ask myself: "What will I be like when I am eighty years old?" I think and hope that I will have loved and known the Lord more and more, that I will have traveled further in the paths of the Spirit, that I will have lived more in the Trinity. Later in heaven that growth will never end; you will continue growing from glory to glory, due to the inexhaustible mystery of God. But having that hunger and thirst now is a grace that comes with the vocation.

3.  I invite you to spend some time thinking about the life of prayer, which is one of the expressions of hunger and thirst for righteousness, or holiness.

    • Examine your fidelity to prayer.
    • Review your life of prayer from the perspective of spiritual growth.
    • Ask for a renewal, a greater thirst, and a deeper hope of growing toward the illuminative life.

Then, examine whether you are growing in the quality of your prayer, and whether your love for Jesus and for the Father is growing through that life of prayer.

In our work with lay people, we want them to experience New Life; not just stick to repeating devotions. Devotions can serve as a first step, but we desire more for others: we long for them to experience and enjoy the Lord in prayer.

Above all, I fervently desire and long for you to have an undivided heart immersed in the things of Christ.

*Glory be to the Father, and to the Son, and to the Holy Spirit. As it was in the beginning, is now, and ever shall be, world without end. Amen.*

# BLESSED ARE THE CLEAN OF HEART

L ET'S continue on to "Blessed are the clean of heart, for they will see God."

Here is another of the commentaries you sent me: "He who has a pure heart seeks God for himself, opening his heart to the Creator; he is authentic, transparent, and capable of entering into intimacy because he works with others and communicates himself exactly as he is. That is why he can enter into intimacy with God, being authentic, pure, and full of integrity, he can have a more profound bond and see more deeply. He is not dulled by the superficial; rather, he sees what is true, which is why he will see God. He doesn't seek approval, doesn't seek his own interests; he is more interested in the glory of God than in his vainglory before creatures."

In this testimony there is a heavy emphasis placed upon transparency, on the authenticity of those persons who seek only the glory of God and the salvation of others. They have no hidden intentions or secret agendas. Therefore, they can enter into intimacy with God and with neighbor. They can establish deeper bonds because they do not hide anything.

In contrast, someone who has a knife hidden in his jacket cannot have this intimacy with others. Because others might discover the knife, he must establish more superficial relationships.

There is a particular beauty in pure hearts. It is easier

for them to discover the continuous and loving presence of God day in and day out, because they see God in each person, as the Beatitude expresses: *They will see God!*

Another testimony says: "It's difficult to choose [one Beatitude to write about], but I went with 'Blessed are the clean of heart, for they will see God' because I want to see God; this desire has always been easy for me to perceive within myself, written on my heart. However, what it means to see God takes on greater significance and reality as I discover his presence through providence in my and others' history, perceive his continuous and loving presence in the day-to-day and live more and more in that presence, and experience powerful moments of prayer on retreats and in the apostolate—particular prayers that come to be true theophanies (revelations). All of that causes the desire for a direct and permanent vision to grow within me. I have also been clarifying over the years what it means to have a pure heart, which at first I reduced to the virtue of chastity. But I have seen that God the Father, Son and Holy Spirit are manifest, are more evident, to those who are clean of heart, without a spirit dulled by sexuality nor dimmed by selfish desires and vainglory, to the simple ones. That is why this Beatitude especially seems to me like Good News, because of the promise it contains."

Someone else wrote: "'Blessed are the clean of heart for they will see God' . . . This Beatitude resonates with me because I associate purity of heart with the purity of chastity, and especially, with the apostle St. John. St. John was young, of low profile compared to Peter. He didn't have a wife. I remember the passage where John is in the boat with Peter, Thomas, Nathaniel—and I believe James—and he was the first to recognize Christ: "It is the Lord!"[1] He was the one who saw him. (I liked this—that it was John who could recognize Christ the most quickly). Also, when he went to the tomb, he realized that Christ had risen. 'He saw and believed.'"[2]

As you can see, all of them have expounded upon the concept of purity, not merely linking it to chastity. It seems to me that the commentaries contain much wisdom.

## The Heart

We're going to go a bit deeper into this Beatitude. First, let's see what "heart" signifies in the Bible. It is the center of the personality, of the sentiments, where the intelligence, will, and feelings are located, including the passions. *Therefore, the heart is not a place but rather a synthesis of the personality.* It is in this sense that the first commandment of the law of God is to "love the Lord with all your heart."[3]

The heart is also a witness to our interior acts, a witness that denounces and makes manifest, as it did to David when he reacted against Saul, who was persecuting him: "So David moved up and stealthily cut off an end of Saul's mantle. Afterward, however, David regretted that he had cut off an end of Saul's mantle. He said to his men, 'The Lord forbid that I should do such a thing.'"[4] Some versions say that David's heart troubled him. In other words, for the

---

[1]    Jn 21:7.
[2]    Jn 20:8.
[3]    Dt 5:5.
[4]    1 Sm 24:6–7.

Bible, *conscience is also the heart, like an interior witness of good and evil.*

Jeremiah declares that sin is "engraved with a diamond point upon the tablets of their hearts."[5] The heart is also the place where, ideally, the divine law is interiorized and accepted. Ezekiel proclaims that, in the future, the law will be written in hearts of flesh and not in hearts of stone.[6]

Now, from the heart proceed both good and evil. Jesus said so very clearly: "From within people, from their hearts, come evil thoughts, unchastity, theft, murder, adultery, greed, malice, deceit, licentiousness, envy, blasphemy, arrogance, folly."[7]

And in the Sermon on the Mount, he says, "Everyone who looks at a woman with lust has already committed adultery with her in his heart."[8] Desiring with the heart does not refer only to a bad thought or a passion, rather more precisely it means to desire with the center of the personality: to desire with my intelligence, will, and feelings. In other words, to make compromises out of weakness and to make a decision about it, even if it remains interior and does not become fact, is to confirm that it happened in the heart where decisions are made, where one's freedom comes into play.

Obviously, being pure of heart—at least in this life—does not mean to be indifferent to the attraction of a particular woman, or to be free from all bad thoughts; that is impossible for all sinful human beings. It goes deeper than

---

[5]     Jer 17:1.
[6]     See Ez 11:19; 36:26.
[7]     Mk 7:21.
[8]     Mt 5:28.

that: it is being capable of so loving Christ that when those affective or carnal temptations happen, they are not within the heart. They are in the flesh, in the imagination, and in the temptations—we live in a very eroticized world—but they do not reach the heart. As the Psalm says, "My heart is steadfast, God, my heart is steadfast."[9]

That is why I state that the heart is the center. Purity of heart implies a purification of the interior, the center of the person.

The one who is pure of heart is full of love of neighbor and love of God, full of charity. He has been touched by the righteousness of God, saved, and grafted onto a new situation, where he is capable of seeing reality as God sees it, of relating to reality as Jesus relates to it.

Those who have a pure heart are blessed because they will see God, not only in heaven, but also now, in this life. They will see God in others and will discover the presence of God in things and events. Blessed are you if you have a pure heart!

*It is important to distinguish between a naïve heart and a pure heart.* Each of us should think of someone that incarnates this Beatitude, as a living example. It might be a priest of the SSJ, or some other priest, or a consecrated person that you know, who is an image of a pure heart. This is not the same as a naïve heart. Naïveté infantilizes us; the pure heart is not the heart of a child that didn't grow up, but rather that of someone who became a child in response to the call of God.

*There is a kind of innocence recovered through a gift of*

---

9    Ps 108:2.

*God—a certain purity for loving and relating to others that
is recovered. It is the cleanness of a sinner who has been
redeemed,* not of an eternal child. At first glance, they
appear alike, but in reality, they are very different. The child
that did not grow up should see a psychologist. Not so the
person who with the grace of God has struggled against
himself and attained a pure heart.

It is always God who purifies us and gives us the gift of
a clean heart; therefore, we have to ask for it with insistence. "Cleanse me with hyssop, that I may be pure; wash
me, make me whiter than snow,"[10] the Miserere says. And
in Revelation, it says, "These are the ones . . . who have
washed their robes and made them white in the blood of
the Lamb."[11] It is the cross of Christ, his sacrifice, which
cleanses us and makes us pure.

When I was young, I knew a priest who sometimes visited our house. His name was Esteban Uriburu. I have a
luminous memory of his presence; he was a man with a
pure heart—one who transmitted that purity of heart—but
he was not a naïve child.

## Celibacy

In the first place, purity of heart refers to the capacity to
love for Christ—with Christ, and in Christ. That is why it
implies transparency and the capacity to relate to others
without hiding anything. Because the pure of heart have a
strong identity, they do not need to live on the defensive.

---

[10]    Ps 51:9.
[11]    Rv 7:14.

Purity of heart is a Beatitude rooted in the virtue of humility. We are all called to have a pure heart.

But now I would like to speak principally to the priests and students of the Saint John Society. We will be discussing celibacy, which can be of interest to anyone who would like to understand the mystery of Christ a little better. But it will chiefly interest those who have received the gift of a vocation to consecrated life.

Celibacy is a special aspect of this Beatitude, because purity of heart is particularly proper to those called to live the kind of life Christ lived, for love of him.

## Celibacy, a Gift of God

*Celibacy is not a price one must pay to be a priest; it is a charism, a gift from God.* Here we will explore why. First—and most importantly, it seems to me—there is a Christological reason for being celibate: because Jesus lived celibately. He chose and embraced that form of life as the one that best expresses the New Life, and his message. In the most radical way, the celibate better expresses, lives, and incarnates:

- the parent-child relationship with the Father,
- fraternity with all people,
- the centrality of the love of God in one's life,
- the orientation toward a mission,
- and the hope of eternal life.

Our constitutions say, "Jesus Christ lived a life completely dedicated to the things of his Father, thus inaugurating celibacy lived for the Kingdom."[12] He inaugurated it and was the first to live it. Jesus was not bound by any ecclesiastical law; nevertheless, he wanted to live that way. He freely chose it.

Newman also chose it, even though he was young and still Anglican.[13] He easily could have married, but he chose celibacy; he chose that lifestyle because he perceived a call to this radicality, distinguishing himself even from the common practice of the Anglican Church. I believe that helped in his conversion; without that choice, perhaps he would not have been as disposed to convert. He might not have had the freedom and dedication to say, *Okay, I will leave everything to take this step.* He would have had many different interests, such as caring for his family, keeping his job position, and preserving a certain kind of lifestyle.

*Celibacy facilitates an undivided heart.*[14] Jesus wanted to

---

[12] Constitutions, #41.

[13] "I am obliged to mention, though I do it with great reluctance, another deep imagination, which at this time, the autumn of 1816, took possession of me,—there can be no mistake about the fact; that it was the will of God that I should lead a single life. This anticipation, which has held its ground almost continuously ever since, —with the break of a month now and a month then, up to 1829, and, after that date, without any break at all,—was more or less connected in my mind with the notion that my calling in life would require such a sacrifice as celibacy involved; as, for instance, missionary work among the heathen, to which I had a great drawing for some years. It also strengthened my feeling of separation from the visible world, of which I have spoken above." John H. Newman, *Apologia Pro Vita Sua.*

[14] "Christ, the only Son of the Father, by the power of the Incarnation itself was made Mediator between heaven and earth, between the Father and the whole human race. Wholly in accord with this mission, Christ remained throughout his whole life in the state of celibacy,

live celibately in order to love the Father with his human heart, in a radical way. He wished to make this love the center of his life, and to love others with an undivided heart.

If Jesus had wanted, he could have married and had children. There would have been nothing wrong with that. But then, how could we feel ourselves equally loved as the children of his flesh? Surely his biological children would have had a different status than we; they would have been in a different category.

Rather, *the love of Christ is deep, personal, and universal in virtue of his complete self-giving. There is not a single human person that can be, in principle, excluded from the love of Christ*; that is why St. Paul says, "There is neither Jew nor Greek, there is neither slave nor free person, there is not male and female; for you are all one in Christ Jesus."[15]

It is true that he had a special closeness with Peter, James, and John, along with the twelve apostles and seventy-two disciples. His human love, as with all human love, was given in concentric circles, but in the heart of Christ there is a place for everyone; his love is inexhaustible. You will not find other loves in Christ, nor other worries and interests. His is the love of a completely unified heart.

---

which signified his total dedication to the service of God and man. This deep concern between celibacy and the priesthood of Christ is reflected in those whose fortune it is to share in the dignity and mission of the Mediator and eternal Priest; this sharing will be more perfect the freer the sacred minister is from the bonds of flesh and blood." Paul VI, *Sacerdotalis Caelibatus*, #21

[15] Gal 3:28.

## Celibate Heart

There are many passages in the Bible about celibacy. Jesus says, "My food is to do the will of the one who sent me and to finish his work."[16] He also spoke of this: "Some are incapable of marriage because they were born so; some, because they were made so by others; some, because they have renounced marriage for the sake of the kingdom of heaven. Whoever can accept this ought to accept it."[17] Not everyone can understand the language that Jesus uses—only those who have received this gift from God.

Jesus further says, "Amen, I say to you, there is no one who has given up house or brothers or sisters or mother or father or children or lands for my sake and for the sake of the gospel who will not receive a hundred times more now in this present age."[18] Here he recognizes a greater self-giving.

When they say to him, "Your mother and your brothers are standing outside," he responds, "Here are my mother and my brothers. For whoever does the will of my heavenly Father is my brother, and sister, and mother."[19] This is proper to a celibate heart: to be capable of loving others to the point of making them mother, brother, and sister.

Jesus is speaking of this concept when he explains the good shepherd: "I am the good shepherd. A good shepherd lays down his life for his sheep."[20] Christ is referring to a

---

16      Jn 4:34.
17      Mt 19:12.
18      Mk 10:29–30.
19      Mt 12:47–50.
20      Jn 10:11.

total offering of one's own life, giving it for those whom one loves.

*Jesus assumed an itinerant and celibate lifestyle; in that way, he became a living icon of the message he proclaimed.* That is why, if we are called to that life, we must live it in Christ and with Christ. We must not only be priests, but we must live like him and configure ourselves to him.

There is a configuration with Christ that only the celibate person can experience.[21] I understand more and more all the time—though never sufficiently—Christ's love for others, because I live this way, as a gift of my vocation. I say "I" in a generic sense, because each of us can experience this. (Later we will look at this more concretely, as it happens to us in daily events.) How can it be that I feel this love for all these people, so different from me in age, in culture—in everything? Sometimes it surprises me.

---

[21]  "Jesus, who selected the first ministers of salvation, wished them to be introduced to the understanding of 'the mysteries of the kingdom of heaven' (Mt 13:11; Mk 4:11; Lk 8:10), but he also wished them to be coworkers with God under a very special title, and his ambassadors (2 Cor 5:20). He called them friends and brethren (Jn 15:15; 20:17), for whom He consecrated Himself so that they might be consecrated in truth (Jn 17:19); he promised a more abundant recompense to anyone who should leave home, family, wife, and children for the sake of the kingdom of God (Lk 18:29-30). More than this, in words filled with mystery and hope, He also commended an even more perfect consecration to the kingdom of heaven by means of celibacy, a special gift (Mt 19:11-12). The motive of this response to the divine call is the kingdom of heaven (*Ibid.* v. 12); similarly, this very kingdom, the Gospel (Mk 20:29-30), and the name of Christ (Mt 19:29) motivate those called by Jesus to undertake the work of the apostolate, freely accepting its burdens, that they may participate the more closely in his lot." Paul VI, *Sacerdotes Caelibatus*, #22.

There is a big difference between the priest—with his particular age and specific context, personality and culture—and the people whom he is sent to serve throughout his ministry.

We are very different. So how do I relate to these youth, these young women, these young men, these people? Why do I have an interest in them? Why do I feel that I am a father to them somehow? Well, that comes through the gift of celibacy; it is Christ in me. If it were not for the gift of Christ's heart, I could not love these people. Do you see? It is Christ in me who takes interest in them. My old self was more limited; he was satisfied with a smaller group of friendships. It is the new man—in other words, Christ in me—who is capable of relating this way. And that mode of relating is a gift, a fruit of celibacy.

I remember the first time I went to HTB church in London to see Nicky Gumbel.[22] It was an ecumenical meeting, so there were pastors, ministers, evangelical preachers, and some Catholic priests. The pastors were there with their wives, the female pastors with their husbands, and we priests were there with each other; we made up a separate group, a group of comrades. In that atmosphere, one could perceive that we were a special group. The pastors seemed to have a certain admiration for the priests, as if they were able to understand and appreciate that there was a greater self-giving and availability among the priests. Some pastors did not seem to notice it, but the more spiritual ones comprehended it. One even told me so; he expressed a nostalgia

---

[22]    Holy Trinity Brompton, the church in London where the Alpha Course, founded by Rev. Nicky Gumbel, began.

for a life lived with the same dedication as Christ had, without other bonds.

So the first reason for celibacy is Christological. Our constitutions draw an analogy between celibacy and prayer life, since both are a participation in the life of Christ. About prayer, they say, "We live our prayer as a grace of participation in the prayer of Christ."[23] And about celibacy, they say, "We ask him to live in us his redemptive chastity, which attains for us union with God on this earth without conjugal mediation and unites us to Christ the Spouse of the Church, allowing us to live as brothers and sisters to all."[24] It is the chastity of Christ, his chastity. And they underline "which attains for us union with God on this earth, without conjugal mediation," because the sacrament of Matrimony is a mediation: the man is a mediation of the love of God for his wife, and vice versa.[25]

---

[23]    Constitutions, #53.

[24]    Constitutions, #42.

[25]    "Matrimony, according to the will of God, continues the work of the first creation (Gen 2:8), and considered within the total plan of salvation, it even acquired a new meaning and a new value. Jesus, in fact, has restored its original dignity (Mt 19:38), has honored it (cf. Jn 2:1-11), and has raised it to the dignity of a sacrament and of a mysterious symbol of His own union with the Church (Eph 5:32). Thus, Christian couples walk together toward their heavenly fatherland in the exercise of mutual love, in the fulfillment of their particular obligations, and in striving for the sanctity proper to them. But Christ, 'Mediator of a supreme covenant' (Heb 8:6), has also opened a new way, in which the human creature adheres wholly and directly to the Lord, and is concerned only with him and with his affairs (1 Cor 7:33-35); thus, he manifests in a clearer and more complete way the profoundly transforming reality of the New Testament." Paul VI, *Sacerdotes Caelibatus*, #20

In contrast, through the gift of celibacy, we are united to God without that mediation; we are united directly to Christ, Spouse of the Church. Jesus is the spouse that gave himself up for the Church—for men and for women—with a faithful, fruitful, sacrificial, and dedicated love.

Therefore, we are placed in the role of the Spouse. We priests are the spouse of the Church in Christ; we are not bachelors or people without commitment.

## Father of Many

A few years ago while living in Córdoba, I traveled to Pilar. My father called to ask me to go to a family reunion that was happening that day. I said, "I'm not going to be able to, Dad." And when he insisted that I be present—as one's parents tend to do—I responded, "Dad, imagine I'm a father with ten kids; I can't go, because I have to take care of ten kids." That argument seemed to convince him.

I think that is a very real analogy, but with even more than ten kids. If a person has more than ten biological children, no one insists that he be present at some birthday or first Communion, and that person's parents do not insist that he come stay the night in their home. No one says to a person who is married with ten children: "Come, stay the night at our home." Quite the opposite! They advise him, "Go, stay the night with your wife." Sure, they invite him to come and visit during the day, but not to leave his own home to sleep in his parents' house. That only happens when marriages are not going well. A married man habitually sleeps in his own home, and not in the home of his parents. I cannot remember a single instance when my parents went to sleep in the house of my grandparents. Well, I think of myself the same way: I am neither single nor separated.

I think that the image of having ten or more kids is very real. This image helps us because it constitutes reality. Priests are called to live like that: as married men and more, because we have more than ten children. It is why we are celibate. If I had wanted to have three or four children, I would have gotten married; I would have loved them, educated them, sent them to a good school, but I did not get married because I wanted to have more children in Christ Jesus.

It allows us to live as brothers and sisters to all. That is proper to the gift of celibacy. If you have a wife and children, it is very difficult for you to live as a brother and friend to all. I see that with great clarity in missionary action. Here there is interest and ability to relate, missionary zeal, attention paid to each individual, the capacity to overcome cultural differences, love for the poor, and a 24/7 investment. Celibacy in Christ makes all this possible.

Later, the constitutions say, "It commits us to a unique relationship of unreserved love with Christ, who offers himself totally to us."[26] Jesus spoke in parables to thousands of people—to all who wanted to listen to him. But he only explained those parables to the twelve apostles. The intimacy of Jesus was with the Twelve. Christ gives himself to us totally because we give ourselves to him totally too. There is a predilection, a complicity, proper to the one who is celibate.[27]

---

[26]   Constitutions, #42.

[27]   "The response to the divine call is an answer of love to the love that Christ has shown us so sublimely (Jn 15:13; 3:16). This response is included in the mystery of that special love for souls who have

## Spiritual Life

The second reason is more practical, and it relates to a greater unity of life. When asked about celibacy and marriage, St. Paul explains in the letter to the Corinthians: *I recommend that you not get married; do as I do, because if you marry, you will have preoccupations, like taking care of your wife and worrying about how to please her. If you want to get married, go ahead and do so. There is no sin in that; it's fine, but . . . I recommend celibacy. You will be able to dedicate yourself more fully to the Lord.*[28] It is a practical argument that he makes here. Furthermore, he is proposing that we have greater unity of life and so be able to busy ourselves exclusively with the things of God.

There is also a reason for celibacy that we could call *ascetic*. The celibate person can develop a deeper spiritual life because celibacy is something like a spiritual gym, and the challenge that accompanies it opens us to a deeper life of prayer.

Married life—with all of its attractions and all of its comforts—anchors the soul more in the body, in a way. Therefore, it does not permit the soul to be so responsive to life lived through the Spirit. Celibate life, in general, allows a greater availability for prayer and a capacity for deeper

---

accepted his most urgent appeals (cf. Mk 1:21). With a divine force, grace increases the longings of love. And love, when it is genuine, is all-embracing, stable and lasting, an irresistible spur to all forms of heroism. And so the free choice of sacred celibacy has always been considered by the Church 'as a symbol of, and stimulus to, charity': it signifies a love without reservations; it stimulates to a charity which is open to all." Paul VI, *Sacerdotes caelibatus*, #24.

[28]     See 1 Cor 7.

listening. Given that human beings are sinners, the dialogue between body and soul is a little damaged. Celibacy better preserves and, if necessary, restores that dialogue.

Buddhist monks, for example, are principally celibate for this "ascetic" reason—in order to dedicate themselves to the spiritual life as they understand it so that their passions do not affect them. I believe I have told you about a conversation I once had with a Buddhist monk, when he visited Argentina. He was a famous monk who gave conferences all over the world, and I was given an audience with him. I went to meet him, and he was very friendly. Conversing with him, I realized that he did not believe in a personal God, but rather in a species of "impersonal totality"; so I asked him why he was celibate. With that perspective, to whom was he consecrating his life? He told me that by definition, human love is a passion.[29] Love, in the end, is reduced to lust, and lust, like any passion, brings suffering; therefore, if you achieve detachment from the passion of love, you will avoid exposing yourself to suffering and will be more free to desire good for all and live in peace. I am not sure if I am doing justice to the thought of this monk, because we spoke for only a few minutes, but I remember that was the impression that stayed with me, and it serves to illustrate what I want to say to you. It seemed to me a very poor reason for living celibately—only as a kind of detachment from the passions. That alone is not enough. *I told him: we want to have a relationship with many people and suffer greatly.* We want to love much, and deeply. That is why we are celibate.

---

[29]     He literally told me: "What's love? Ultimately, love is lust."

And then there is a more "logistical" reason, connected to our missionary mobility. Our lifestyle is forged from the image of the public life of Jesus, who was itinerant and totally available to others.

It is true that there are married priests in the Eastern Catholic Church; but it is also true that the church that goes out—as Pope Francis says, the missionary Church—has always been the Western Church. The church that has penetrated all cultures, and has had that absolute availability to go out, is the Church that counts on celibate priests.

## "Lord, I Have Given You Everything"

Being called to the priesthood is a gift; for through this gift, we are admitted into the community of the Twelve, to the love of Christ without conjugal mediation. We are bonded with the heart of Christ, allowing us to love the Father and to love others as he loves them. We also are allowed to be fathers in him.

This gift introduces us to the priestly life through the call of Jesus; without this gift, celibacy is impossible. At best, abstinence could be possible through a great effort of will. But fruitful celibacy is a gift of God; that is why it requires a charism—a calling. For that reason, it must be received with humility, as an unmerited gift. Having received that charism does not mean we are better, rather that we have been mysteriously chosen.

One of the signs of a vocation is that the person grows in this; not only in that from which he abstains—which is only a part—but also in his capacity to take charge of others and establish bonds, to give himself to the loves of Jesus, to love others whom he might not love if he were not celibate, and, *in Christ*, to take interest in those in whom he ordinarily would not. That is the gift of celibacy. Others become important to me personally because "it is no longer I who live, but Christ who lives in me."[30]

However, this can imply a real and costly renunciation at times. *It is a call to a higher lifestyle; it is the one that Jesus chose, but it still requires renunciation.*

This renunciation is of something good and attractive, which is also anchored in one's own flesh. There is the renunciation of intimacy with a woman, of that exclusive bond and the affection and tenderness that a woman gives you; there is a renunciation of sexual pleasure and of having one's own biological family. Without a doubt we are speaking of costly renunciations.

But one gives these things up through the awareness of a personal calling. Renunciation takes letting go and mourning, saying: *This is good, lovely, and attractive, but it is not what I chose; it is not my calling, not what God asks of me.*

At times we have the mistaken idea that we only have to renounce what is evil in itself, only renounce sin. But that is not true: there are things that are good in themselves that we are called to renounce due to our choice of other things that we want more.

## There Is a Renunciation

The love of Jesus, and the love of the Father and of our spouse, the Church, does not replace the personal experience of the

---

[30]     Gal 2:20.

love of a woman, for it is not exactly the same. It is a different love—deep, and very capable of gladdening the heart of man—but not the same. That is why there is a renunciation involved, which must be maintained and renewed over time. It is a positive thing because it is a way of reminding ourselves, of saying as Peter did, *Lord, I have given you everything... Yes, Peter, I already know, and that is why you will sit with me in my kingdom; I already know, Peter, that you have given everything.*[31] The Lord sees this.

The other day I was thinking about those who give this up for other lesser reasons: for example, those in the military who go off to war and leave their home and their family. They do this for something of lesser importance than the kingdom of heaven: the good of the country, which is important but less valuable. Another example might be a rural teacher who makes her students her family.

It is good to remember that we are not the only ones who renounce such things. There are other people who have made that renunciation for something they considered a good more valuable than themselves. We renounce a lesser good for the sake of something still greater; and though it is a greater good, it still involves sacrifice.

### Exercise

I suggest that you pray in three parts.

1. Let the first prayer be of thanksgiving for this call—for this gift. *I thank you, Lord, that you have called me to*

---

[31]    See Mt 19:27–30.

*follow you like the Apostle John.* Thank God for the gift of being able to love that which he loves.

2. Secondly, look inward to your heart and ask for the grace to be able to let go of whatever Jesus is asking you to renounce. If you receive that grace, renounce those things even more deeply and offer them to the Lord.

3. Finally, ask for a vision of the future, of how your celibate heart is going to develop over time: *Lord, if I grow in this calling that you give me, where will it lead my heart? What will it mean in my life to grow continually purer of heart?* Ask to see how your heart will advance as you move deeper in renunciation for Christ.

*Glory be to the Father, and to the Son and to the Holy Spirit, as it was in the beginning, is now and ever shall be, world without end. Amen.*

# BLESSED ARE THE MERCIFUL

## Jesus Reveals the Human Face of the Merciful God

"**B**LESSED are the merciful for they will be shown mercy."[1] The Gospel is filled with examples of this Beatitude. Many are the parables in which Jesus insists that we must forgive in order to be forgiven,[2] or practice mercy in order to be received into heaven.[3]

Aware of the prominence of mercy in the Gospel, St. John Paul II wrote an encyclical dedicated to the mercy of God (*Dives in Misericordia*). In this encyclical, he says that the mercy of the Father for men—and of men for each other—constitutes the essence of the evangelical ethos.[4] *It is the heart of the Gospel; God is merciful because he turns toward his entire creation gratuitously, with a love that is not from necessity, but is pure gift.*

The Incarnation speaks to us of the mercy of God. In the canticle of Zechariah and in the canticle of the Blessed Virgin—canticles that proclaim in praise the mystery of the Incarnation—it is made manifest that mercy is the reason God became man.

Zechariah says, ". . . *because of the tender mercy of our*

---

[1]    Mt 5:7.

[2]    See Mt 18:23–35.

[3]    See Mt 25:31–46.

[4]    John Paul II, *Dives in Misericordia*, 3.

*God,* by which the daybreak from on high will visit us to shine on those who sit in darkness and death's shadow, to guide our feet into the path of peace."[5] Earlier he had also said, "... *to show mercy* to our fathers and to be mindful of his holy covenant."[6] The Virgin Mary says, "*His mercy is from age to age* to those who fear him."[7]

*The Incarnation shows us that God is rich in mercy, and that he goes out to meet us. He meets us in our weakness, in our fragility, in our broken situation. He goes out to rescue us. Therefore, Jesus is merciful and reveals the human face of the merciful God, in his life and in his works.*

*Christ has an inexhaustibly merciful attitude toward sinners* and those who suffer, the sick, those who are far away, and lepers. He cites the Old Testament twice when he says, "If you knew what this meant, 'I desire mercy, not sacrifice' ..."[8] and admonishes the Pharisees, "Do you still not understand?"[9] He reproaches them for their lack of mercy and demands much of them.

In the Gospel, Jesus is always seen as understanding with the weak yet as demanding—even indignant—toward those who lack mercy.

## The Mercy of God Rejoices When the Sinner Draws Near

Christ is compassionate with the sheep who have no shepherd,[10] and in his preaching and teaching, he frequently

---

5.  Lk 1:78–79.
6.  Lk 1:72.
7.  Lk 1:50.
8.  Mt 12:7.
9.  Mt 9:13.
10.  See Mt 9:36.

expounds on the topic of mercy. In Luke 15, we have the parables of the mercy of God in which Jesus, with images that are already a common patrimony, speaks of the mercy of the Father.

In the famous parable of the prodigal son, it is moving to contemplate the father who, when he saw his son from afar, was so moved that he ran to meet him, embraced and kissed him, placed a ring on his finger and sandals on his feet, killed the best lamb, and threw a party.[11] Notice how many details attempt to express the mercy of the Father toward the sinner. It is a text to ruminate over. *How many times have we heard it, but still find it hard to believe in the mercy of a God that rejoices in such a way for the sinner who draws near and is reached by salvation!*[12]

The parable of the shepherd who leaves the ninety-nine sheep in order to seek the one who was missing is also poignant; when he finds the lost sheep, he carries it on his shoulders. Jesus says, "I tell you, in just this way, there will be more joy in heaven over one sinner who repents than over ninety-nine righteous people who have no need of repentance."[13] And in the parable of the lost coin, a woman sweeps her house, finds the lost coin, and throws a party.[14] For God, each one of us is this recovered coin!

On the other hand, Jesus is indignant with cruelty and hardness of heart. For example, in the parable of the two servants, after one is forgiven an enormous debt, he is

---

[11]  Lk 15:11–32.

[12]  St. Faustina compared the sin of the world to a drop of water, that had been submerged in the ocean of Divine Mercy.

[13]  Lk 15:7.

[14]  Lk 15:8–10.

unwilling to forgive a much smaller debt of a fellow servant. He is then severely punished by the master who had forgiven him in the first place: "'You wicked servant! I forgave you your entire debt because you begged me to. Should you not have had pity on your fellow servant, as I had pity on you?' Then in anger his master handed him over to the torturers until he should pay back the whole debt."[15]

Jesus goes out to meet the sinner and rescues him, as he did with the adulterous woman. There, at the insistence of the Pharisees, he proclaims, "Let the one among you who is without sin be the first to throw a stone at her."[16] With Zacchaeus, he is also merciful. Though Zacchaeus is a tax collector, Jesus enters his house and proclaims there that he has been saved, rescued for the kingdom.[17]

## Mercy for Judging

During the Sermon on the Mount, Jesus further develops the Beatitudes by teaching mercy instead of judgment: "Stop judging, that you may not be judged. For as you judge, so will you be judged, and the measure with which you measure will be measured out to you. Why do you notice the splinter in your brother's eye, but do not perceive the wooden beam in your own eye? How can you say to your brother, 'Let me remove the splinter from your eye,' while the wooden beam is in your eye? You hypocrite, remove the

---

[15]    Mt 18:32–34.
[16]    Jn 8:7.
[17]    Lk 19:1–10.

wooden beam from your eye first; then you will see clearly
to remove the splinter from your brother's eye."[18]

In Matthew 18, Jesus does teach about the necessity of
fraternal correction, particularly within the Christian community;[19] but in the Sermon on the Mount he is speaking
about judgment of the heart that condemns the other. This
judgment looks at the other, not with love or friendship,
but with condemnation. That is why the constitutions say,
"We know how to forgive and to seek forgiveness, trying to
eliminate any harsh sentence from our judgment and any
resentment from our heart."[20] What do the constitutions
mean by the word "harsh"? It means a condemnation, a
conclusive judgment, from which it is difficult to redeem
oneself. Mercy knows how to discover, see, and value the
best in the other. Mercy bows before others' difficulties and
suffering out of compassion; it has the capacity to suffer
with the other, to be at his side, to help him. That comes
from God. Harsh, rash judgments are opposed to mercy.

---

[18]     Mt 7:1–5.
[19]     "If your brother sins [against you] go and tell him his fault between you
         and him alone. If he listens to you, you have won over your brother. If
         he does not listen, take one or two others along with you, so that 'every
         fact may be established on the testimony of two or three witnesses.' If
         he refuses to listen to them, tell the church. If he refuses to listen even
         to the church, then treat him as you would a Gentile or a tax collec-
         tor. Amen, I say to you, whatever you bind on earth shall be bound in
         heaven, and whatever you loose on earth shall be loosed in heaven." Mt
         18:15–18.
[20]     Constitutions, Est. 63.

## Merciful Love

Another important teaching of the Sermon on the Mount is love for one's enemies. "You have heard that it was said, 'You shall love your neighbor and hate your enemy.' But I say to you, love your enemies, and pray for those who persecute you, that you may be children of your heavenly Father, for he makes his sun rise on the bad and the good, and causes rain to fall on the just and the unjust alike. For if you love those who love you, what recompense will you have? Do not the tax collectors do the same? And if you greet your brothers only, what is unusual about that? Do not the pagans do the same?"[21]

Love of one's enemies has always been considered a specifically Christian characteristic. Our natural inclination is to pay back what we have received—to return it, as if we were a mirror. If we have received indifference, we return indifference, and so on. But that dynamic does not work with the love of our enemies.

*Merciful love goes beyond simply mirroring back what we have received; rather we project, illuminating others with the mercy we have received from God.*

When we have not forgiven our enemies or those whom we feel contradict us—"enemies" is a strong word and not always applicable in our daily life—it is hard for us to pray. Our lack of mercy is an obstacle to prayer and experiencing the mercy of the Father. That is why Jesus says, "When you stand to pray, forgive anyone against whom you have a

---

[21]   Mt 5:43–47.

grievance, so that your heavenly Father may in turn forgive you your transgressions."[22]

God is merciful; he loves with a merciful love, is compassionate and slow to anger, says the word of God.[23] Jesus is also merciful: he goes out to meet the suffering and weakness of each sinful human being. Christ both practices and teaches mercy, and through his teaching and example, he invites us to be merciful too.

John Paul II, in *Dives in Misericordia*, writes:

> Based on this way of manifesting the presence of God who is Father, love and mercy, Jesus makes mercy one of the principal themes of his preaching. As is His custom, He first teaches "in parables," since these express better the very essence of things. It is sufficient to recall the parable of the prodigal son, or the parable of the Good Samaritan, but also—by contrast—the parable of the merciless servant. There are many passages in the teaching of Christ that manifest love-mercy under some ever-fresh aspect. We need only consider the Good Shepherd who goes in search of the lost sheep, or the woman who sweeps the house in search of the lost coin. The Gospel writer who particularly treats of these themes in Christ's teaching is Luke, whose Gospel has earned the title "the Gospel of Mercy."[24]

Luke is very much surprised by this feature in the life and teaching of Jesus, and he transmits it well in his Gospel.

## Mercy in Action; Jesus as Missionary

I would like to end the commentary on this Beatitude with two points that seem especially relevant to me.

---

[22]   Mk 11:26.

[23]   "The Lord, the Lord, a merciful and gracious God, slow to anger and rich in kindness and fidelity." Ex 34:6.

[24]   John Paul II, *Dives in Misericordia*, #3.

First, a very concrete environment where we can practice mercy is in our common life, in the house where each of us lives now. There our capacity to forgive, to avoid rash judgments and condemnation, and to be good, understanding friends with one another, is put into practice each day.

At times God allows us to experience—in our own flesh—weakness, and even sin. And sometimes it can seem that he takes his hand from us so that we may fall. We remember, for example, when God said, "I will make Pharaoh so obstinate"[25] so that he would not let the people of Israel leave Egypt. Without a doubt it is somewhat paradoxical, but it alludes to this mysterious reality: on occasion, God hardens our heart. In other words, he helps us less and leaves us to our own obstinate and hard hearts. Then we may fall, and there . . . we learn to be more merciful!

That is the good that God brings out of evil; he allows us to crash and burn in order to teach us that we are not as holy or as good as we think. On the contrary, we are sinners, but forgiven by the grace of Christ, and that is why he invites us to be merciful with our brothers. If we truly want God to help us, let us practice mercy, drawing near and helping one another, without condemnation.

St. Thomas writes, commenting on Aristotle, "Men pity such as are akin to them, and the like, because it makes them realize that the same may happen to themselves. This also explains why the old and the wise who consider that they may fall upon evil times, as feeble and timorous persons, are more inclined to pity: whereas those who deem themselves happy, and so far powerful as to think themselves

---

[25] Ex 14:4.

in no danger of suffering any hurt, are not so inclined to pity."[26]

The person who believes himself to be strong, powerful, and successful, tends to be harder with others because he cannot imagine himself in the same situation of necessity . . . until he later needs others!

Now, we don't need to hope to be in a poor situation. If things go well for us, if we are successful, if life smiles on us, we can be even more merciful so that God may continue blessing us!

The second point to remember is that the habitual way that we live mercy is in the apostolate. *As missionaries of the New Evangelization, we go out and seek those baptized who do not know Jesus Christ, through the power of the Holy Spirit. That is a work of mercy—the most important one of all.*

I would like you to reflect on this bond. God is merciful and goes out to meet man; the Son is incarnate and reaches his hour, going around to all the towns and cities announcing the Good News of the kingdom,[27] searching for sinners. That is mercy in action. *The mercy of God in action is Jesus the missionary.* So his mercy is shown through teaching and calling.

It happens in us in the same way. "Call, form, send,"[28] are actions of Christ, who is the one who calls, forms, and sends. We are moved by mercy, by the merciful love of God who goes out to meet the one who does not participate, the

---

26  St. Thomas Aquinas, *Summa Theologiae*, II–IIae – q. 30, a. 2c.

27  See Mt 4:23 and 9:35.

28  "Call, Form, Send," are three words that describe the missionary itinerary of the Saint John Society's programs of evangelization.

one who does not feel himself called and maybe does not even know that he has been called.

*Merciful love does not depend on what the other gives us in return, but rather demands that we take the initiative. This is essential to mercy: merciful love has its own drive.*

There are other loves that rely upon a give and take. But the love of the missionary is a love that gives, sows, goes out in search, calls, and gathers.

This is our strongest work of mercy—the one we do time and time again: the apostolate. We are missionaries!

We configure ourselves with Jesus in his public life in order to preach the same message he did. In those three years, Jesus proclaimed a message—Good News—that some time later was written down in the New Testament. That message is synthesized in parables, the Sermon on the Mount, his teachings, and in each one of the gestures and attitudes of Christ.

The letters of St. Paul and the rest of the writings of the New Testament amplify and echo that message. In Christ there is a New Situation, a novel ingredient, a breakthrough that transforms us through a relationship of merciful love into children of the Father.

Pope Francis emphasizes that mercy is a central aspect of the message of Christ, and that is why he wanted to proclaim a Jubilee of Mercy. The pope writes, "Jesus Christ is the face of the Father's mercy. These words might well sum up the mystery of the Christian faith. Mercy has become living and visible in Jesus of Nazareth, reaching its culmination in him."[29]

---

[29]    Pope Francis, *Misericordiae Vultus*, #1.

He further proposes mercy as an essential attitude for the New Evangelization:

> In the present day, as the Church is charged with the task of the New Evangelization, the theme of mercy needs to be proposed again and again with new enthusiasm and renewed pastoral action. It is absolutely essential for the Church and for the credibility of her message that she live and testify to mercy. Her language and her gestures must transmit mercy, so as to touch the hearts of all people and inspire them once more to find the road that leads to the Father. The Church's first truth is the love of Christ. The Church makes herself a servant of this love and mediates it to all people: a love that forgives and expresses itself in the gift of oneself.[30]

So, we have to understand and interpret mercy just as Jesus understood it in his public life: as a paternal solicitude of God toward sinners, toward those who are far away, toward the poor. It is also a zeal to reach everyone with the Good News of the love of the Father, who is rich in mercy. It is a missionary mercy, a fire that Christ has come to bring to the earth.[31]

*In summary: for the Saint John Society, the most important, most urgent, and most necessary work of mercy is the New Evangelization.*

We do not always link mercy to apostolic zeal, but it is very important for us to do so, as that link exists and is real. At times when I'm in the Newman Center, I think: *All of these students here do not know Jesus Christ, and their lives are going to be without him, with all that entails. If they get married without Jesus Christ, they may divorce, as so many*

---

30    Ibid., #12.
31    "I have come to set the earth on fire, and how I wish it were already blazing!" Lk 12:49.

*do; they might become materialistic and individualistic; they will live without Jesus Christ and die without Jesus Christ.* And I feel a deep mercy, a huge desire to proclaim Jesus Christ to them. Because if they receive him, their lives are going to be something completely different.

Can you see how *the Beatitudes are like a spiral? They do not address separate topics, but are related to each other and deepen each other mutually, as they reflect the living heart of Christ.* All of them speak of love, of the apostolate; each point is related. We separate them in order to consider, reflect on, and pray with each one.

## Exercise

1.  Contemplate Jesus, full of mercy, going out to evangelize. You can use the text of Jesus's first preaching in Nazareth:

    He came to Nazareth, where he had grown up, and went according to his custom into the synagogue on the sabbath day. He stood up to read and was handed a scroll of the prophet Isaiah. He unrolled the scroll and found the passage where it was written: "The Spirit of the Lord is upon me, because he has anointed me to bring glad tidings to the poor. He has sent me to proclaim liberty to captives and recovery of sight to the blind, to let the oppressed go free, and to proclaim a year acceptable to the Lord." Rolling up the scroll, he handed it back to the attendant and sat down, and the eyes of all in the synagogue looked intently at him. He said to them, "Today this scripture passage is fulfilled in your hearing."[32]

---

[32]   Lk 4:16–21.

You can also reflect on point 12 from our constitutions:

This Christ evangelizer and preacher lives in us, not only because we preach the Good News in His Name, but also because we preach Him, and doing so requires an intimate knowledge of Jesus and a full configuration with Him. "What we have seen with our eyes, what we have looked upon and touched with our hands, concerning the Word of life . . . we proclaim it to you now,"[33] the apostle John said.

2.  I also invite you to examine the works of mercy that the *Catechism of the Catholic Church* enumerates:

The works of mercy are charitable actions by which we come to the aid of our neighbor in his spiritual and bodily necessities (cf. Is 58:6–7; Heb 13:3). Instructing, advising, consoling, and comforting are spiritual works of mercy, as are forgiving and bearing wrongs patiently. The corporal works of mercy primarily consist of feeding the hungry, sheltering the homeless, clothing the naked, visiting the sick and imprisoned, and burying the dead (cf. Mt 25:31–46). Among all these, giving alms to the poor is one of the chief witnesses to fraternal charity; it is also a work of justice pleasing to God (cf. Mt 6:2–4).[34]

The practice of the works of mercy is an essential aspect of the formative path for lay people; that is why in the constitutions of the ASJA (Association of Saint John the Apostle), it says, "Every member of the ASJA will have a sensitivity and particular interest for the poor. This preoccupation will be seen, in the first place, in their treatment of the poor around

---

[33]   1 Jn 1:1.
[34]   CCC 2447.

them, and also in a collaboration with some work of service to the community, be it explicit evangelization or social action; we call this the 'plus of a noble cause.'"[35]

I invite you to relate these works of mercy to your life and apostolate, and to ask Christ to give you a heart full of mercy.

*Glory be to the Father, and to the Son, and to the Holy Spirit, as it was in the beginning, is now and ever shall be, world without end. Amen.*

---

[35]    ASJA Statutes, #16.

# BLESSED ARE THE PEACEMAKERS

## Producer of Peace

THE original Greek used for this Beatitude is *"eirene poios,"* which means a worker for peace, a laborer for peace, or an artisan of peace. Some Bibles translate it: "blessed are the peaceful," but the original word has a specifically active intention: *artisans, producers, or projectors of peace—people who facilitate peace wherever they may be, who not only have peace, but radiate it.* That is why they will be "called children of God," because peace is, in a way, the New Situation. We know that peace in Hebrew is said as *"shalom,"* which has a very rich resonance in the Bible; it is the fullness of blessing that a man can desire for himself and others in this life. It is peace with God, peace with others, fullness of life, and serenity.

Therefore, the one who works for peace is not merely one who avoids conflict—in that case it would be someone peaceful and, at most, meek—but rather one who experiences the peace that comes from God and is rooted in justice, in the New Life. It is he who will be called a child of God because he helps spread the peace of God throughout the world.

## Servants of Reconciliation

Jesus Christ is the one who brought peace. He has reconciled us and, as St. Paul says, made us ministers or servants of the reconciliation of human beings with God and one another. The Second Vatican Council affirms that this is precisely the purpose of the Church and why it was instituted by Jesus: to be a facilitator of union between men and God and, therefore, among men.[1]

But let's tackle this topic of peace in two more specific points.

## Fraternal Peace

First, fraternal peace: above all, in the community. This Beatitude does not principally allude to a natural disposition, such as a mellow temperament, but rather to conduct in the community in which charity is spread, the bonds of friendship and fraternity are established, and broken bonds are restored.

From the perspective of Matthew's Gospel, the first beneficiaries of this search for peace and reconciliation are the members of the Church. When Matthew writes these texts, he is thinking of the challenges facing the newborn Church;

---

[1]  "Since the Church is in Christ like a sacrament or as a sign and instrument both of a very closely knit union with God and of the unity of the whole human race, it desires now to unfold more fully to the faithful of the Church and to the whole world its own inner nature and universal mission. This it intends to do following faithfully the teachings of previous councils." *Lumen Gentium* 1 (http://www. vatican.va/archive/hist_councils/ii_vatican_council/documents/ vat-ii_const_19641121_lumen-gentium_en.html).

that is why he reminds them of the teachings of Jesus and, inspired by the Holy Spirit, offers them as the Word of God for the Church.

It seems to me that some particular texts in the Bible can help us reflect on this. For example: "If there is any encouragement in Christ, any solace in love, any participation in the Spirit, any compassion, any mercy . . ."² St. Paul is saying: *If you would listen to me, please, if what I have to say matters to you, if Jesus Christ rose and is truth, if he is really present in the Eucharist, if you have faith and are Christians, then listen to what I am going to say.* He continues, "Complete my joy by being of the same mind, with the same love, united in heart, sharing the same thoughts. Do nothing out of selfishness or out of vainglory; rather, humbly regard others as more important than yourselves, each looking out not for his own interests, but for those of others."³

*"Do nothing out of selfishness or out of vainglory." What practical advice this is, and how important for common life!* We are all tempted by vanity or vainglory.

Humility brings us to esteem others as superior, not only as equals . . . and how far we are from this humility! That is why we have to ask for it: *Lord, give me a true vision of things.* Seeking the interest of others means, among other things, overcoming the temptation to be self-serving or to take advantage of others.

---

²     Phil 2:1.
³     Phil 2:2–3.

### Rising to the Level of the Calling

Let's dig into two texts that echo these themes. The first text I recommend for your reflection is in the letter of St. Paul to the Ephesians.[4] First Paul says, "I, then, a prisoner for the Lord, urge you to live in a manner worthy of the call you have received," which is a way of saying: *Rise to the level of your calling.*

Then he continues, "*with all humility and gentleness, with patience, bearing* with one another through love, striving to preserve the unity of the spirit through the bond of peace." *He does not say a little, but all humility; all the Beatitudes come into play.*

Next he uses a very realistic expression: "*Bearing* with one another through love." At times we must put up with each other. As young people say: *I'm here for you, no matter what; I'll put up with you even today, when you're being a bit difficult. I don't know what's going on, but I'll hang in there with you.*

Paul also insists on the same thing in the letter to the Colossians:[5] "Put on then, as God's chosen ones, holy and beloved, heartfelt compassion, kindness, humility, sweetness, and patience, bearing with one another and forgiving one another, if one has a grievance against another; as the Lord has forgiven you, so must you also do." Be merciful, and you will be shown mercy.

"And over all these put on love, that is the bond of perfection." *The bond of perfection—the bond of New Life—is*

---

4     Eph 4:1–4.
5     Col 3:12–15.

*love. There is no other bond of perfection; though there may be other bonds, they are not perfect.*

"Let the peace of Christ control your hearts, the peace into which you were also called in one body." This is the peace of which the Beatitude speaks, a peace in which we form one single body. It is the peace of Jesus.

Humility, sweetness, and patience. Sweetness is opposed to bitterness, the trait of one who is always complaining and in a bad mood. Sweetness is proper to a person that has light. This is the first dimension of peace: seeking peace in the community.

## Malleability

Another aspect of this first reflection is peace toward the large community of the church, for which we need malleability. In other words, we need the capacity to establish relationships with very different groups and people within the same Church. This is very important for us because we are missionaries, and many times we take on the leadership of works that are already in process: for example, a parish that is already functioning, or a Newman Center that already has a history.

When we arrived at one Newman Center, the woman in charge had a very different vision from ours of how the work with university students should be. We thought in very different ways. There was also a pastor whose vision was very different from hers and very different from ours. So from the beginning there were three very different styles in play.

Not only that, but in the parish there was a group very

sensitive to doctrinal orthodoxy. They called themselves "the pillars of truth," alluding to the expression of St. Paul.[6] And, well, each group wanted us to get on board with their vision. It required a great deal of flexibility to say, "I'm not going to get involved in battles that are not mine; rather, I am going to proclaim Jesus Christ. I don't want to waste energy on whether I'm associated with one group or another, or get involved in internal battles that—though they may be important—are not ours. *We will do our part, and our part is to proclaim Jesus Christ; that is what is essential.*"

Malleability consists in this: it is the ability to be a force of peace. It is something that all involved at this parish recognized with time: that we could speak with everyone, that we worked with both Hispanics and students, and that we wanted to dedicate ourselves to what is essential when faced with the whole world.

*And that is why we could bring peace, because we Christians unite in what is essential:* love for Christ and the certainty that in him there is a New Situation.

Another example I remember is when Fr. Guillermo arrived at the parish in Montevideo and encountered a few people who had been there for years; for that reason they had a very determined idea about "how things had always been done." When we met with them, I was struck by how much and how well Fr. Guillermo took each one into account. He did not exclude them; rather, he listened to them and still does, which makes him a force of peace.

We do not arrive and begin from scratch. *Our style is*

---

6    "You should know how to behave in the household of God, which is the church of the living God, *the pillar and foundation of truth.*" 1 Tm 3:15.

*to **assume** what is already there, **purify** it, and **elevate** it. For that to happen, a certain malleability is necessary: the capacity to distinguish the essential from the accidental and to determine which points we cannot compromise.* There will always be essential things to fight for, but there will certainly be others where we can be flexible, in order not to waste energy on minor skirmishes.

A fundamental requirement for having this malleability, which is also prudence, is solid formation. Solid intellectual formation gives you malleability. If you have four or five truths hanging by a thread, well, then you cling to these and you become very rigid. On the other hand, if you enter into an eclecticism without solidity—a destructive relativism—you become salt without savor and a dimmed light. If you have a solid formation, that formation allows you to distinguish with prudence. As St. Thomas Aquinas said in his articles, *Oportet distinguere* (*It is important to distinguish*).

### Personal Peace

Now there is a second meaning of peace on which I would like to reflect, and that is personal peace.

Being a peaceful person and cultivating this personal peace implies combatting anxiety. I want to say some words on anxiety, because it is a danger that stalks people with many responsibilities—those who are very busy, with many things to do.

It is a danger that shadows missionaries, too, because in our life there is always less time than one would like to have. If we live our self-giving well, there is little time for being bored.

There are always books to read, people to call, apostolates to organize and manage, prayers to pray; time is always too short. It would be a bad sign to be a missionary who gets bored and doesn't know what to do. I don't believe that happens to you. It doesn't happen to me, either.

Without a doubt, anxiety is a danger for busy people.

One of our priests wrote to me, commenting on this Beatitude:

> He who improves in the ways of the Spirit, whether he be consoled or disconsolate, has to guard his peace of heart . . . not allowing anything to steal it . . . When you are rushed, you need to say to the Lord, "Keep me in your peace." I think this must be the "guarding of the heart" about which the desert fathers spoke. Even when you are fighting against temptations, you must not let anything steal peace from your soul.[7] That is why, I think, after the Our Father, the Holy Mass invokes, with exorcism, the liberation from all distress, and we immediately offer one another the PEACE of Christ.

## About Anxiety

I googled the word "anxiety" and found this definition: "A mental state characterized by a great disquiet, an intense agitation and extreme insecurity."[8]

How accurate!

Disquiet, agitation, insecurity . . .

---

[7]   *"Conquer peace (with the help of the Lord) and a thousand people around you will find salvation."* St. Seraphim of Sarov. / *"The enemy of our souls will seek to combat all forms of spiritual joy by introducing SADNESS and PERTURBATION into us."* (Spiritual Exercises 329. St. Ignatius of Loyola).

[8]   https://es.oxforddictionaries.com/definicion/ansiedad, Translation mine.

Disquiet: I sit down to read, but instead think about how I have to organize some meeting . . . I want to organize, but I answer an email . . . I pray, but in reality, I am mentally planning my agenda . . . I plan my agenda, but I can't finish because I already started to speak with the first person on my list . . . I speak with that person but don't listen to him; I just look like I'm listening. Disquiet does not let us enjoy what we do, because we are already thinking about what is to come, about the next thing.

Agitation: speeding up. Some symptoms are: speaking too much, running from one thing to the next, being out of alignment, eating too much, and devouring my food.

Insecurity: I propose visualizing the image of a three-year-old child that is all wound up and over the top. The father comes in, picks him up, embraces him, and murmurs: *Shh, quiet down.* The child relaxes, because he is with his daddy.

Anxiety takes root in the fear that something will go wrong, and from that fear follows the need to be affirmed. Consequently, our fear leads to seeking the value of our life in achievements, in hyperactivity, in the certainty that one has worth because one is living to the extreme. That is why many times we say things like "*I am burnt out, tired, exhausted, stressed, overwhelmed, busy . . .*" and other such things, which sometimes are meant to make others notice how much we do and how busy we are. Others also give that back to us: *I know you don't have a spare minute . . . I know you have a very busy schedule . . . with everything you do . . .* This gratifies our ego.

A little acceleration in our lives is understandable and can be tolerated or accepted. We are founding a society. We share this foundational impulse. We have to open paths, establish houses, develop communities and programs, work for vocations, form them and care for them; we have to reach those who are far away from God and the Church and prepare something attractive and appealing for them. All of this we generally do with pleasure, with a passion for the kingdom that is truly evangelical.

I am proud to belong to the Saint John Society. We are sacrificial, hard-working, upright, and tough. We manage many things, have holy ambitions, and have a high level of faith. If we fail in an apostolate, we try from a different angle, until things go well. This is because we have received the gift of evangelizing.

But that passion for the kingdom, if not channeled well, converts into anxiety and degenerates into mere activism. If it is transformed into a vice, then it becomes extremely difficult for us to slow down. That hyperactivity turns against what we want to achieve, which is to announce the Good News of the kingdom with all of its fruits—one of which is peace, the serenity of knowing ourselves loved by Christ gratuitously and unconditionally.

Fr. Raniero Cantalamessa writes:

> The effort for a renewed missionary commitment is exposed to two principal dangers. One is inertia, laziness, not doing anything and letting all the others do the work. The second is launching into feverish and futile activity on a merely human level, resulting in losing contact little by little with the wellspring of the word and its efficacy. This would be setting oneself up for failure. The more the volume of activity goes up, the more the volume of prayer should go up. One might object that this is absurd because there is only so much time. That is true, but cannot the one who multiplied the bread also

multiply time? This is something God is always doing and
that we experience every day: after having prayed, we do the
same things in less than half the time. One could also say, "But
how can you remain praying and not run when the house is
on fire?" That is also true. But imagine this scenario: a team
of firefighters who hear an alarm rush with sirens blaring to
where the fire is. However, once there, they realize they do not
have any water in their tanks, not even a drop. That is what we
are like when we run to preach without praying. It is not that
the words are lacking; on the contrary, the less one prays the
more one speaks, but they are empty words that do not reach
anyone.[9]

What can we do? How can we make good concrete use of
time and give every last minute, without running in vain?
I'd like to share with you ten suggestions taken from different conversations I have had throughout the years, ranging
from the more spiritual to the more practical. *You can use
them as a decalogue for attaining greater peace.*

## 1. Nourish Your Deepest Identity

The first and most important step is to nourish your deepest
identity: *In Christ, I am a child of the Father.* Return to this
truth in prayer, especially when you are anxious, rushed,
afraid, insecure, or anguished. And do it in real time: in
that moment, become aware and pray, *I am a child of the
Father.*

I'd like to use an image that I've used earlier: that of the
floodgates that open into the canals. I learned about this
concept in Villa Dolores, where they water the fields by
using canals. From the dike, some canals run toward the

9    Raniero Cantalamessa, Third Lenten Homily, 2016.

fields, watering them along the way. The system is managed by floodgates, which open and close according to a predetermined schedule so that the water is directed to one canal or another. The owners of the fields rent scheduled time for the floodgates to open into their canals. I am sure that the system is a bit more sophisticated than that, but I am describing it simply.

Well, something like that happens in our heart. We have a source: Jesus, who is compared to a fountain of living water.[10] The presence of Christ in us is like a fountain that springs up to eternal life. It is the stream of water in the image described by the prophet Ezekiel:[11] the water flows from the temple, which is Christ in us, and waters all the land until it reaches the sea and restores our shores. That is the image of the New Life. It springs from the heart, because it is in the heart that we are united to Christ as he permeates our intelligence, our will, our feelings, our affections, and even our body.

But that is one fount; the other source of water is the old self that is also there. There are two canals: the canal that is the presence of Christ in us and the canal that is the old self, and they both give water. At times, the water that flows is that of the old self, which overflows some of our canals in a disorderly way.

So what can we do in the moment when we realize what is happening?

We have to close one floodgate and open the other. When we realize that the old self is dominating us, that we

---

[10] See Jn 7:38.
[11] See Ez 47:1–12.

are insecure, or feel afraid, uneasy, anguished or anxious, we first need to become aware of what is happening, stop for a second, and go to close one floodgate and open the other.

In other words, go to the heart and say, "Lord, you are in me! Right now, I am a little agitated, rushed; I am full of interior noise, but I want to close this floodgate from my old self and open yours. I need *your humanity to arise in me, your peace to flow in me; give me your peace.*" The Risen Lord Jesus promised it and gives it: "Peace I leave with you; my peace I give to you."[12] *Give me your peace, I am a child of the Father. That is our deepest truth.* We take a minute to enter into communion with the heart of Christ, to open that door and let that living water flow and penetrate our humanity in that moment.

We can, for example, repeat words from the Gospel, because *those words are charged with and penetrated by the Holy Spirit,* and they come to our aid. Lately, I have been repeating often: "Good and faithful servant."[13] That phrase helps me; I like pondering it because I believe that it is a phrase that the Lord says to each one of us. The word of God is like a whisper that we can interiorly evoke until the Holy Spirit lifts up that interior repetition and anoints it with his presence, helping us realize that it really is true. Let us seek to nourish our deepest identity.

Let's say that you have to take a test. Well, close your eyes for a few minutes and water the field of your humanity

---

12    Jn 14:27.
13    Mt 25:21.

with the presence of Christ in you. Do it just like that with whatever you have to face.

Stop for a moment and direct yourself to your deepest identity to restore your peace again. Who are you? Where are you going? Who is your Father? Are you an orphan, or are you a child of your Father? Feed that fountain; let the Living Water flow through you. It might take you two or three minutes to do this, but you will gain much more because you will be acting in the peace of God.

On the other hand, it is also important to humbly seek that affirmation from your superiors: "Give me a blessing, because I am feeling a bit nervous and rushed."

I remember one time when I had to give a talk in a Fragua, on the Holy Spirit Weekend, and I felt unconfident, not because of what I had to say, but because of my English. I was afraid I wouldn't be able to do it well. I had eighty young people before me ready to listen, and I was thinking: "It's going to go poorly; I'm going to get stuck; I won't be able to do it."

We all know how young people are: they don't give you much room for error. Maybe two or three minutes, if they are generous, but if you don't hook them in that time, they won't pay much attention. Fr. Ignacio was there, and I said to him, "Ignacio, I am nervous; give me a blessing because I need you to help me preach in English." He blessed me and that helped a lot. It took some humility to do it, but later I preached well, with serenity.

We all have to face situations like that, and to do so, we need humility.

Human beings naturally live beneath the gaze of authority.

Some of you have told me: "I don't live beneath the gaze of God. It matters a lot to me what a certain person thinks," or what anyone thinks, whichever superior or whichever person has a certain authority, "it matters to me." I do not think there is anything wrong with this mattering to you; I think it is natural and even good. To a soldier, it matters what his general thinks, and to a soccer player, it matters what his coach thinks. There is something pure in that. To a child, what his father or mother thinks matters to him, because he loves them, and they constitute a real authority.

So you cannot expect to live in a filial relationship with God—mediated by human authority—without anything else mattering. If you want nothing else to matter to you, it is better that you live alone, but if you live in community, you will certainly care about the opinions of those in authority over you. This is just something you must accept.

Now, this fact does not have the last word. Behind all of it, I can see the presence of God. He is the one who gives meaning to all authorities, who are all mediators. It is important that we reflect on this from the perspective of a child of God: *I am a child of God, and I see the bond that exists between him and the person that has human authority over me. I see with clarity where that authority comes from.* Does that help you understand?

The pretense that it doesn't matter to me what an authority thinks is a rationalization that is not constructive. Human beings are in relation with one another, and we influence each other. Such is life, and it's how God made us. In the world, people have to be accountable to someone, even though in the end we will find ourselves before God.

So it is fundamental that we work on that identity: *I am a child of God; I am a missionary; I am a member of the Saint John Society, I'm not in this alone.*

What is my deepest and most consistent identity? I am the favorite child of the Father in Christ Jesus. I am his missionary. His body and his blood enter into me every single day.

Father, here I am, working like a mule, the best that I can: you know this. Here I am, with a thousand weaknesses, too, but my heart is yours: you know this also. Tell me, Father, the words that I need to hear. My worth is not in what I do but in the fact that I am your child. You don't need my work, but you offer me participation in your saving plan for the world, through pure love of predilection. Even if I fail, you will carry out your work. So I give you what I have, and I will be at peace. I don't seek my glory but your glory, Lord! Not to us, but to your Name give the glory, Father.

I remember a text from Newman: "I have my mission; I am a link in a chain, a bond of connection between persons. He has not created me for naught. I shall do good; I shall do His work; I shall be an angel of peace, a preacher of truth in my own place."[14]

God knows who I am. He never walks away in defeat; I have to give him my trust.

## 2. Be Present in What I Do

This is ancient spiritual advice!

For this, we have to be resolute and ascetic in our

---

[14]	John Henry Newman, *Meditations and Devotions*, (San Francisco: Ignatius Press, 1989), 383.

decisions. The other day, I was on the San Juan Diego retreat for women, accompanying 118 women. As there is everywhere, there was Wi-Fi. At the beginning, I faced a choice: I could completely enter into the retreat, be present for the talks, imbibe the spirit of the retreat, listen to the testimonies, pray, intercede, confess, preach, etc., or I could escape with my computer to answer email and work on overdue projects, then appear like a cuckoo to give my talk, confess at the scheduled time, and celebrate the Mass.

This second scenario was tempting, because it was less affectively and spiritually demanding and more relaxing physically. But after thinking about it for a couple of minutes, I dove into the retreat. It was a grace. Not only could I be present in the retreat, but I could also give better advice. When I preached, I knew who I was speaking to and could really put my heart into it, leaving behind the manual and speaking with my whole self. I could also enjoy the whole weekend. I saw the glory of God acting in the life of those women. At the end, I was filled with joy, tired but renewed in spirit . . . with a great unity of heart. There wasn't even much need to recollect myself; it was enough just to rest a little more the next day. Being fully present in what I do is a good deal!

At the beginning of something, two doors always open: either I can be completely present in what I undertake, or I can merely be a person who is "wintering" there. The first is more demanding, but it makes me imitate Jesus and truly enjoy it. The second turns me into a functionary of the faith, so criticized by Pope Francis.

He writes:

We are speaking of an attitude of the heart, one which approaches life with serene attentiveness, which is capable of being fully present to someone without thinking of what comes next, which accepts each moment as a gift from God to be lived to the fullest. Jesus taught us this attitude when he invited us to contemplate the lilies of the field and the birds of the air, or when seeing the rich young man and knowing his restlessness, "he looked at him with love" (Mk. 10:21). He was completely present to everyone and to everything, and in this way, he showed us the way to overcome that unhealthy anxiety which makes us superficial, aggressive, and compulsive consumers.[15]

This applies to study, spiritual direction, the team meeting . . . or cleaning the bathroom. It means to put my heart all in and accomplish what I have to do, guided by a schedule that is inspired by what God wants from me. I will speak more about this a bit further on.

### 3. Ask Yourself: Is There Something From Which I Am Escaping?

Many times, anxiety arises from not facing something with clarity. Let's suppose there is something which worries me: it might be a pending obligation, a decision that I have to make, a person who is not well, an exam.

I recently heard some advice that can help with respect to this, and it consists in setting a determined time and space—for example, half an hour in the chapel or at my desk—to "worry" about that topic. For example, if I have to make a decision, then I decide that I will do so on Thursday after thinking about it for half an hour in the chapel.

---

[15]     Pope Francis, *Laudato Si'*, # 226.

Until then, I will try not to keep it on my mind constantly, because life must go on!

It also might be that I am hiding from some personal question—something that I have been sweeping under the rug for some time. Suppressing such questions is neither constructive nor conducive to peace. Facing them and responding to them is what brings peace. Avoiding topics, putting them off for later—not as a free decision, but as an escape—not only generates anxiety but also brings you to very destructive evasions.

I could also be avoiding my spiritual lukewarmness, my lack of growth. I run because I am not finding pleasure in being with the Lord; I don't see occasions for growth; I am in a routine, stagnant relationship. Or I cannot enjoy reading some spiritual book or being in silence. All of this could lie beneath the deceptive mantle of being very occupied, very busy.

## 4. Cultivate Friendship

True friendship is a fount of serenity because it is gratuitous. Gratuity calms anxiety. Fr. Vallés once told a story about how when he was given an important literary prize for one of his books; his anxiety began to grow. It was a book about spiritual peace, but the fame, the editorials that they offered him for the next book, the invitations to conferences filled him with anxiety.

With the next book, he had still more success and more anxiety. And so he entered into a cycle he couldn't escape. Perturbed and dejected, he went to speak with another Jesuit who had been his friend since their time in seminary.

This Jesuit, after kindly listening to him, told him, "Don't worry about me, I've never read your books." In other words, we are friends not because of your success, fame, or books; rather, we are friends, period. It is a gratuitous friendship, in which one can find support.

## 5. Have a Schedule Inspired by This Mission

Create a schedule that is realistic and inspired by what we are and what we want to be. If your daily schedule says that you are going to go for a run each day for an hour, well, that is a bit extravagant because you are not preparing to be a marathon runner, but a priest. *Your schedule has to be in accordance with your identity; it has to reflect what you are, what you want to be, and what God is calling you to be.* A schedule helps a lot, without a doubt. And it implies an ascetic of "no" and an ascetic of "yes:" knowing how to say "yes" and "no" in keeping with what we believe we have to do.

## 6. Confirm the Schedule With One Who Has Authority

Run it by the rector: "What do you think? Do you agree with these priorities?" We need the support and confirmation of our superiors. We have not come to do our own will but rather to do what God wants for each one of us. We have not come to be served but to serve. We all desire that. Therefore, it is important—to have the blessing of God and to have the peace of one who is obedient to another—that the rector see our schedule, bless it, and support it. Later, be faithful to it. Sustain it. Remembering the phrase from the Gospels, "Let your yes be yes and your no, no,"[16] will be helpful for this. Obedience is essential to our path. Superiors have the grace to help us discern the paths of God, to steer us away from self-gratification, and guide us to the glorification of God with our actions. They help us know how to say "no," how to cut, and how to prioritize. Certainly, we need humility to consult and ask for light, but peace is born from obedience and humility.

## 7. Leave Room for the Unforeseen

Now, as much as we want to be faithful, it is also necessary to leave space for the unforeseen.

We cannot expect to depend upon our schedule in the same way as a monk, whose routine is repeated with exactitude each week. It is necessary for us to have a schedule, but also to know that a certain dynamic flexibility is needed— it's a missionary's schedule!

Things that come up and require our attention also come from God, so we must accept them with peace. If I want to do what God asks of me, this is not a problem. A rapid discernment is needed, in the moment. This thing that has come up, that presents itself to me, is it merely a distraction, the fruit of my interior anxiety, a circumstance that can wait? Or do I really need to let go of what I am doing or had planned to do and engage in this unforeseen thing?

To decide, you must stop for a couple of minutes. Breathe deeply, put yourself in communion with the heart of Christ, and discern. These are two valuable minutes that

---

[16]    Mt 5:37.

permit us to do what is best, in the best way. Later, if it is possible, recover the time for what is a priority by subtracting it from what is secondary. If that is not possible, holy peace. Next week will be better! What cannot be done, will not be done. If God does not want it, neither do I. He is the one in charge.

### 8. Have Daily, Weekly, Monthly, and Annual Rhythms

Sometimes what cannot be done within the week, can be done within the monthly rhythm. It is helpful to look to the horizon, not just at the day to day.

### 9. Rest. Sleep the Necessary Amount of Time

Habitually sleeping too little causes a rush, as if the body needs to go at a forced march, and that dulls us spiritually. Nowadays the value of rest is well known, the value of the body-soul-spirit harmony, of serenity and interior silence.

In other words, we cannot give a testimony of spirituality or demonstrate that we are moved by the Holy Spirit if we are exhausted or stressed or rushed. It is not an attractive or luminous testimony.

All of those who radiate fatherliness possess a certain serenity of spirit, which cannot be attained if one does not rest enough. One might wonder if we must fight against laziness, but I don't believe that is a danger for us right now.

## 10. Exercise

Even if we are tired, we need to exercise. It is an investment of time and energy that results in a greater physical and emotional well-being. It's like sharpening an ax: you have to stop a moment to do it, but later it cuts more effectively.

Going for a run is very helpful. It is a gratifying sport that can be done in any free moment. In one hour, it is possible to go for a run, come back, shower, and be ready to do something else. You can run while listening to Christian music or simply in silence, and you can run wherever you are. I believe the key is to continue running until you learn to enjoy it, as happens with every art.

Eating healthily also helps. Besides fasting, it is best to avoid heavy foods, which leave you sleepy and too full for spiritual things. The monks understood this, which is why asceticism constitutes a fundamental part of the Christian tradition.

***

We embrace a demanding life. "Holiness rather than peace," was John Henry Newman's motto. I believe it is important to accept that a little stress is the salt of life. We come to the Saint John Society to give of ourselves—to live "nearly consumed" for the kingdom.

In no way do these words aim to feed an individualistic spirit, centered on our own psycho-emotional wellbeing. Rather, the aim is to maximize the resources at our disposal in order to deploy a better evangelization. It is fidelity to the truth: to the truth of God and of myself, of the vocation and the gift of grace.

St. Francis de Sales wrote in *The Introduction to the*

*Devout Life*, "Similarly, when we are worried and tired [anxious], we lose our power to maintain the virtue that we had acquired. We also lose the means for resisting the temptations of the enemy who then makes every effort to fish, as they say, in agitated waters." Also: "Anxiety is the deadliest thing that can happen to us, with the exception of sin."[17]

It is evident that one will have to sleep little some nights, to fast, to make demands of the body and of the spirit as Jesus did, who forgot to eat because he was attending to the people. But he also sought times for prayer or for getting into the boat with his disciples and sailing the sea. Even the popes rest!

It is not an evasive rest, nor one unrelated to the mission, but is rather the rest of a warrior, who rests that he might be able to fight the next battle.

And at the resurrection, the most precious gift Christ gives us is peace. "Peace be with you!"[18]

St. Paul testifies that for Christ, he passed through "***toil and hardship, through many sleepless nights,*** through hunger and thirst, through frequent fastings . . . and apart from all these things, there is the daily pressure upon me of my anxiety for all the churches."[19] We also have to be ready to pass through these and other difficulties so that the Good News can reach all those whom Christ allows us to reach.

St. Paul also writes, "Rejoice in the Lord always. . . . Have

---

[17]  I recommend reading the chapters about inquietude and about sadness, chapters 11 and 12 of the fourth part of *The Introduction to the Devout Life*.

[18]  Jn 20:19.

[19]  2 Cor 11:27–28.

no anxiety about anything . . . make your requests known to God. Then the *peace of God* that surpasses all understanding will guard your hearts and minds in Christ Jesus."[20]

## Exercise

I invite you, now, to pray with these three topics:

1. The first is fraternal peace: Let us pray to be people of peace toward the community, to be facilitators of peace. Let's not think only of being peaceful, but of promoting unity, friendship, and reconciliation. It is important to know how to praise others, how to speak in a way that eases and dissolves tension, how to tell a joke at the right moment. Let us ask Jesus that we not be divisive, but that we be peacemakers. Let us look to Christ who tells us, "Blessed are the peacemakers."

2. The second: Let us renew our desire to study and to be formed in order to have prudence and malleability.

3. The third is personal peace and anxiety: Let us pray to be renewed in our deepest identity and *to let the water of the presence of Christ flow in us in order to obtain that peace of God.*

*Glory be to the Father, and to the Son, and to the Holy Spirit, as it was in the beginning, is now and ever shall be, world without end. Amen.*

---

[20]     Phil 4:4–7.

# BLESSED ARE THEY WHO ARE PERSECUTED

## The Joy of Persecution

THIS Beatitude says, "Blessed are they who are persecuted for the sake of righteousness, for theirs is the kingdom of heaven."[1]

It's interesting that it specifies those who are persecuted *for the sake of righteousness*: they are not persecuted for intemperance or for stupidity, not for being uselessly rigid, bad-humored or unjust, nor for being mediocre, clumsy, imprudent, or so many other possibilities, but rather for righteousness.

That is why, in his first letter, the apostle Peter writes, "Beloved, do not be surprised that a trial by fire is occurring among you, as if something strange were happening to you." In other words, don't think it is strange; it is not something extraordinary. That is why he insists, "But rejoice to the extent that you share in the sufferings of Christ, so that when his glory is revealed you may also rejoice exultantly. If you are insulted for the name of Christ, blessed are you, for the Spirit of glory and of God rests upon you." Then he clarifies, "But let no one among you be made to suffer as a murderer, a thief, an evildoer, or as an intriguer. Whoever

---

[1]    Mt 5:10.

is made to suffer as a Christian should not be ashamed but glorify God because of the name."[2]

I think that *when you can't comprehend why someone is persecuting you, whether it be personal or institutional, it is a healthy attitude not to completely dismiss the possibility that that person or that institution might have some reason for it.*

It is good to first be self-critical: *Let me see . . . have I been intemperate, lukewarm, or whatever they are accusing me of being?*

It is not constructive to quickly label yourself a victim. In my experience, when there is criticism and incomprehension, there tends to be some (and sometimes a lot of) reason behind it. It is good to listen first with humility and, when appropriate, correct oneself. If not, it is very easy to polarize things, making yourself out to be this persecuted saint and everyone else to be your evil persecutors.

Usually things are not so simple as we make them out to be, and we all have our pride, self-love, errors, and sins. That is why you first need to listen, consider, pray, and correct yourself. If, after this exercise, one finds before God that the criticism is unjust or disproportionate, well, rejoice and be glad. Because it was already written that it would be this way.

## Jesus Announces Persecutions and Exhorts Us to Persevere

Nevertheless, Jesus has announced many times the possibility of being persecuted: "Watch out for yourselves. They

---

[2]  1 Pt 4:12–16.

will hand you over to the courts. You will be beaten in synagogues. You will be arraigned before governors and kings
because of me, as a witness before them. But the gospel
must first be preached to all nations. When they lead you
away and hand you over, do not worry beforehand about
what you are to say. But say whatever will be given to you
at that hour. For it will not be you who are speaking but the
holy Spirit. Brother will hand over brother to death, and the
father his child; children will rise up against parents and
have them put to death. You will be hated by all because
of my name. But the one who perseveres to the end will be
saved."[3]

Strong words, right?

The other day I read a commentary by Bishop Robert
Barron, Auxiliary Bishop of Los Angeles, about the failure
of the Supreme Court regarding the constitutional right to
gay marriages.

Without diving too far into the topic, his point is that
declaring gay marriage to be a constitutional right means
that any conscientious objection to that right, whether it
be a judge or a school or a mother giving her child up for
adoption who wants the adopting couple to be heterosex-
ual, could be persecuted or labelled as narrow-minded, a
fanatic or bigot. It is not difficult to see the potential persecution of Christians by a relativistic and secularized culture.

In any case, Jesus already predicted it. This persecution
has happened throughout the twenty centuries of the history of Christianity, especially in the twentieth century,

---

[3]    Mk 13:9–13.

which produced the most martyrs of all time.[4] So we have to be ready for it. Right now, in the twenty-first century, we are seeing the testimony of the martyrs of the Middle East, persecuted by ISIS.[5]

This train of thought should not lead us to fight daily battles that are not ours, or get lost imagining possible future martyrdom. But it is good to become aware of the heroism and faith of many Christians today. Two examples are Cardinal Stepinac, who was in prison for five years in Yugoslavia, and Cardinal Van Thuan, who spent thirteen years in jail, nine of them in isolation.

With so many examples of heroic people who have suffered persecution for years, one has to think: *If one day I*

---

[4]     As an example, this should be enough: "The figures from Spain are huge, but pale before what we know from other places, above all from Russia. In Spain 12 successive bishops were assassinated for being bishops. In Russia 250 orthodox bishops, bishops in apostolic succession, were killed. If in Spain 7,000 priests and religious were assassinated for being such, in Russia the numbers are truly terrifying: 200,000 members of the clergy and religious (bishops, priests, monks, deacons, and nuns) were assassinated between 1917 and 1980. And between 1937 and 1938 alone, in Russia some 165,100 orthodox priests were arrested, of which 105,000 were killed. The figures can be found in the precious book of Andrea Ricardi titled, *The Century of the Martyrs*, published in Barcelona in 2001." Juan Antonio Martínez Camino, Auxiliary Bishop of Madrid, oral presentation during 'Diálogos de Teología 2014', Facultad de Teología de Valencia.

[5]     Pope Francis said, with respect to the Christians beheaded by ISIS in Libya, "*We offer this Mass for our 21 Coptic brothers, beheaded for the single fact of being Christians. We pray for them, so that the Lord receive them as martyrs, for their families and for my brother Tawardros who suffers so much.*" The 21 martyrs died pronouncing for the last time the words, "Lord Jesus Christ," sealing their martyrdom and their trust in the victory of Jesus Christ.

*have to face something like that, I know God will help me.*
We cannot totally remove from the horizon the possibility
of giving testimony to Christ to the point of persecution or
even martyrdom.

### Following Christ Is Being Open to Suffering Persecutions

Before reaching such extremes, there are other subtler types
of persecution which might be closer to our experience.
They are what some call the "persecution from the good":
persecution that comes from within the Church. This could
be a certain misunderstanding or tenacious opposition
from people who think they are doing their duty when they
criticize, persecute, or complicate things for you. This happens because sometimes God allows it.

Being open to and facing these tests is proper to new
foundations. We recently began our activity in a certain
diocese, and thanks be to God, things are going very well;
the bishop and the priests received us with joy, and the people too. Praised be to Christ who helps us!

But it could also happen that some priest criticizes us,
that someone else disagrees with our way of approaching evangelization, or that someone thinks we should not
receive so much support from the bishop because we are a
new group coming in from outside, etc. It seems to me that
in the beginning, you have to be open to the possibility that
someone might not like what you do or how you do it. They
may not understand it, and therefore they might criticize it.

We need to know this could happen and do all that is
necessary to prevent it: cultivate good relations, participate

in all the meetings, be prudent. No one in the Church wants persecution, no one ever looks for it, and we must try to avoid persecutions. But if they come, meet them with faith—after ruling out our own errors, as I said before.

God willing, you too will face the same situation: opening a new SSJ house, being in a new place, having to start from the beginning. Well, that is probably going to require facing some hostility.

*The only way to avoid persecution is by doing nothing.* If things don't go well for you, if people don't respond to your call and invitations, if your apostolates fail and you don't have new vocations, if no one helps you economically and no one goes on your retreats or converts, you will arouse more pity than persecution.

But if you do well and people convert, if they help you economically, if you have vocations and the results of your missionary action are visible, many people will support you and others will criticize you. You have to be willing to meet conflict if it arises. *If your primary concern is to avoid conflicts, then many things will never come to pass. As we know, avoiding conflict never was the primary concern for Jesus.*

I invite you to live these issues with a spirit of faith and to prepare yourself, tighten your seatbelt. You cannot follow Christ if you are unwilling to face certain misunderstandings and persecution.

Some in the Church may criticize or oppose you, so as to sanctify you through the providence of God, but that same Church also blesses you and opens new horizons to you!

It is through the Church that we have houses in Uruguay, the United States, Italy—that we are in any place at all. The Church is the one that provides you with structure, helps and connects you. It is by the authority of the Church that you are sent, that you arrive in a place and begin to work. And the people trust you because you are a mission-ary—one who is sent. But every now and then, they shake you so that you remember with humility who you are. In the providence of God, everything works for the good of Christians if we accept it with faith.[6]

There can also be some misunderstandings that are more domestic in nature. I always like to tell this story about Fr. Flavio:

Once, when we were still in the seminary, as we were coming back from working with the bees, a priest corrected him for having cut a plant in the wrong season. I was beside him, and he didn't say a word. Later, when the priest had left, I asked Flavio why he had cut the plant in the wrong season. I was astonished when he told me he hadn't been the one to cut it.

"So why didn't you tell him that it wasn't you?" I asked.

"Why defend myself?" was his response. "Someone cut the plant, so the priest was right. He told me and that's it. What's the problem? Why should I defend myself in some-thing that is so unimportant? The priest was right; he was angry because the plant was cut. Another seminarian cut it, but he blamed me. Perfect, problem solved."

I always remember that moment because it is not so easy to accept a correction when you are not the one who com-mitted the fault, is it? It is even more difficult to do it with humility and joy. But training yourself in this way will help

---

6       "We know that all things work for good for those who love God, who are called according to his purpose." Rom 8:28.

you understand a little better what it meant for Jesus to take our place—the innocent for the guilty.

If from time to time you suffer some misunderstanding or injustice in community life, if someone thinks something of you that isn't true, well, it's not necessary that you staunchly defend your honor or your name. Occasionally it might be necessary, but most of the time it is not.[7] And on these occasions, the exercise of remaining silent can help you grow in humility. This is also useful in family life.

### Exercise

1. I encourage you in this last meditation to say to the Lord: *Lord, if I have to face some persecution, injustice, or difficulty for practicing righteousness, you can count on me. And if it is not for the sake of righteousness, but due to my own fault, help me to repent, change, and be more prudent next time.*

2. Next, I encourage you to read and pray with this famous page from the *Little Flowers of St. Francis of Assisi*:

One day in winter, as St Francis was going with Brother Leo from Perugia to St Mary of the Angels and was suffering greatly from the cold, he called to Brother Leo, who was walking on before him, and said to him: "Brother Leo, if it were to please God that the Friars Minor should give, in all

Jesus said to St. Faustina, "Strive to make your heart like unto My humble and gentle Heart. Never claim your rights. Bear with great calm and patience everything that befalls you. Do not defend yourself when you are put to shame, though innocent. Let others triumph. . . . I Myself will speak up for you when it is necessary." *The Diary of Saint Maria Faustina Kowalska*, (Stockbridge: Marian Press, 2016), 1701.

lands, a great example of holiness and edification, write down, and note carefully, that this would not be perfect joy." A little further on, St Francis called to him a second time: "O Brother Leo, if the Friars Minor were to make the lame to walk, if they should make straight the crooked, chase out demons, give sight to the blind, hearing to the deaf, speech to the dumb, and, what is even a far greater work, if they should raise the dead after four days, write that this would not be perfect joy." Shortly after, he cried out again: "O Brother Leo, if the Friars Minor knew all languages; if they were versed in all science; if they could explain all Scripture; if they had the gift of prophecy, and could reveal, not only all future things, but likewise the secrets of all consciences and all souls, write that this would not be perfect joy." After proceeding a few steps farther, he cried out again with a loud voice: "O Brother Leo, thou little lamb of God! If the Friars Minor could speak with the tongues of angels; if they could explain the course of the stars; if they knew the virtues of all plants; if all the treasures of the earth were revealed to them; if they were acquainted with the various qualities of all birds, of all fish, of all animals, of men, of trees, of stones, of roots, and of waters—write that this would not be perfect joy." Shortly after, he cried out again: "O Brother Leo, if the Friars Minor had the gift of preaching so as to convert all infidels to the faith of Christ, write that this would not be perfect joy." Now when this manner of discourse had lasted for the length of two miles, Brother Leo wondered much within himself; and, questioning the saint, he said: "Father, I pray thee teach me wherein is perfect joy." St Francis answered: "If, when we shall arrive at St Mary of the Angels, all drenched with rain and trembling with cold, all covered with mud and exhausted from hunger; if, when we knock at the convent-gate, the porter should come angrily and ask us who we are; if, after we have told him, 'We are two of the brethren,' he should answer angrily, 'What ye say is not the truth; ye are but two impostors going about to deceive the world, and take away the alms of the poor; begone I say'; if then he refuse to open to us, and leave us outside, exposed to the snow and rain, suffering from cold and hunger till nightfall—then, if we accept such injustice, such cruelty and such contempt with patience, without being ruffled and without murmuring, believing with humility and charity that the porter really knows us, and that it is God who maketh him to speak thus against us, write down, O Brother Leo, that this is perfect joy. And if we knock again, and the porter come out in anger to drive us away with oaths and blows, as if we were vile impostors, saying, 'Begone, miserable robbers! Go to the hospital, for here you shall neither eat nor sleep!'—and if we accept all this with patience, with joy, and with charity, O Brother Leo, write that this indeed is perfect joy. And if, urged by cold and hunger, we knock again, calling to the porter and entreating him with many tears to open to us and give us shelter, for the love of God, and if he come out angrier than before, exclaiming, 'These are but importunate rascals, I will deal with them as they deserve'; and taking a knotted stick, he seize us by the hood, throw us on the ground, roll us in the snow, and beat and wound us with the knots in the stick—if we bear all these injuries with patience and joy, thinking of the sufferings of our Blessed Lord, which we would share out of love for him, write, O Brother Leo, that here, finally, is perfect joy. *And now, brother, listen to the conclusion. Above all the graces and all the gifts of the Holy Spirit which Christ grants to his friends, is the grace of overcoming oneself, and accepting willingly, out of love for Christ, all suffering, injury, discomfort and contempt;* for in all other gifts of God we cannot glory, seeing as they proceed not from ourselves but from God, according to the words of the Apostle, '*What hast thou that thou hast not received from God? And if thou hast received it, why dost thou glory as if thou hadst not received it?*' But in the cross of tribulation and affliction we may glory, because, as the Apostle says again, '*I will not glory save in the cross of our Lord Jesus Christ.' Amen.*"[8]

---

[8]    *The Little Flowers of St. Francis.* Garden City: Hanover House, 1958. p. 319.

3.  Finally, consider Cardinal Merry del Val's wise and healing *Litany of Humility*. When I first read this, I was twenty-one, and I liked it so much I glued it into my Bible. I have never moved it, because I would like to have it always present, to help me be free from myself.

Jesus, meek and humble of heart: hear me.
(To each of the following, respond, "deliver me, Jesus.")
From the desire of being esteemed,
From the desire of being loved,
From the desire of being extolled,
From the desire of being honored,
From the desire of being praised,
From the desire of being preferred to others,
From the desire of being consulted,
From the desire of being approved,
From the fear of being humiliated,
From the fear of being despised,
From the fear of suffering rebukes,
From the fear of being calumniated,
From the fear of being forgotten,
From the fear of being ridiculed,
From the fear of being wronged,
From the fear of being suspected,
That others may be loved more than I, Jesus grant me
    the grace to desire it.
That others be esteemed more than I, Jesus grant me
    the grace to desire it.
That, in the opinion of the world, others may increase
    and I may decrease, Jesus grant me the grace to
    desire it.
That others may be chosen and I set aside, Jesus grant
    me the grace to desire it.
That others may be praised and I unnoticed, Jesus grant
    me the grace to desire it.

That others may be preferred to me in everything, Jesus
   grant me the grace to desire it.
That others may become holier than I, provided that I
   may become as holy as I should, Jesus grant me the
   grace to desire it.

Pay close attention: *From the fear of being humiliated, deliver me, Jesus; from the fear of being despised,
deliver me, Jesus; from the fear of suffering rebukes,
deliver me Jesus; from the fear of being calumniated,
forgotten, ridiculed, wronged, suspected . . .* They are
all persecutions, right?

*Free me from that fear, Lord. Do not let me so seek
to avoid these situations that I leave undone any good
I should do. Let me live face to face with the Father, in
view of the mission that you have given me, with the
prudence and astuteness of the children of light.*

*Glory be to the Father, and to the Son, and to the Holy
Spirit, as it was in the beginning, is now and ever shall be,
world without end. Amen.*

# THE BEATITUDES AND
# THE MESSAGE

## A Message That Reflects the Face of Christ

THROUGHOUT history, problems have arisen with the interpretation of the Sermon on the Mount. Due to the radicality of some of these affirmations, many have challenged them and asked themselves: where will these lead us if we take them seriously—*if we always have to turn the other cheek, if we always have to walk that extra mile?* The questioning isn't only directed at the Sermon on the Mount but also at other similar teachings in the Gospel that are in conformity with it.

But the truth is that, while it is difficult to condense the Sermon on the Mount into just one idea, if we could speak of a profile, an "ethos," a kind of music that arises from the reading of these texts, it would be the face of Christ; this presents a challenge to be accepted and experienced in one's own life.

There is an interior battle waged by our old self, which resists embracing the face of Christ reflected in the Beatitudes. Jesus says, "I am the way";[1] we have to walk with him on the path to reach the Father, and that path is Christ's humanity, patterned after the Beatitudes and the Sermon

---

[1]    Jn 14:6.

227

on the Mount. There is no other path besides his humanity, with all those specific traits that are his, but also ours.

I think the reason that sometimes we feel an interior rebellion against the Sermon on the Mount and its teachings is that we don't want to be poor, or meek, or merciful, or pure, or persecuted, but rather completely the opposite. We want to be powerful, brilliant, admired, praised, strong, superior to others; we feel a strong temptation to be diametrically opposed to the way proposed in the Beatitudes. *Our interior self can set out on a warpath against this program that is the essence of the Gospel.*

Sometimes this temptation is even thrown at us by that same one who tempted Jesus in the desert: "Then he took him up and showed him all the kingdoms of the world in a single instant. The devil said to him, 'I shall give to you all this power and glory; for it has been handed over to me, and I may give it to whomever I wish. All this will be yours, if you worship me.'"[2] The temptation can arise violently and unexpectedly. *Satan cannot understand the Sermon on the Mount; it seems like nonsense to him and he despises it and all those who want to live it.* He despises Jesus Christ even while he fears him. And he hates man.

It is so important, when you realize the origin of this temptation, to react with determination: *Get behind me, Satan!* Don't engage in dialogue but rather seek light in the teaching of Christ, which is the rock upon which one can construct the house of his life.[3]

This is why I want to stress to you that neither the

---

[2]    Lk 4:6–7.
[3]    See Mt 7:24–27.

Sermon on the Mount nor the Beatitudes are programs for the fainthearted. *It is not a weak teaching nor a teaching for the weak. Very much the opposite: it requires a lot of strength and love and a gift from God to apply the Beatitudes to our lives.*

These teachings embrace suffering, practice chastity as a strong love, and bear persecution with joy, because they have as their goal a kingdom that is higher—one that is won after a long combat and only by the grace of God. They are not for the pusillanimous but rather for the magnanimous. These teachings don't quarrel with leadership but rather purify the root of leadership and put it to service for following Christ.

Deep down, the rejection of the Sermon on the Mount is a rejection of Jesus Christ. And the world rejects Jesus Christ, either because they don't understand him or because they consider him utopian, inapplicable, or weak. Once, a person told me, "My problem with Christianity is not its ethic but rather its aesthetic. I don't understand it; I prefer war, political struggle, the fight that rewards the strongest."

But the world isn't stronger; it is more violent, yes, but it's not stronger. *Strength is not the same as violence. Jesus is strong without being violent; he is one who works for peace. Strong is the one who believes, while violent is the one who destroys. God is strong.*

## The New Situation in the Face of the Sermon on the Mount

As you may remember, some time ago I asked you for exercises before beginning the retreat. I'd like to share with you now some excerpts from a few of those exercises you sent me. I liked them a lot!

The first links the Sermon on the Mount with the New Situation and says:

> The one who has discovered the New Situation is transformed into a light for others; but that light should not be hidden. He must go out to illuminate, to proclaim with his life. This is what is seen in people who have had a deep encounter with Christ. They discover the spirit of the Law. They don't follow the Law just because it is a Law—like a burden—but rather they count on the grace that surpasses the Law and goes beyond it. They have encountered the love of God which moves them to give a response of love that surpasses the Law.
>
> The one who discovers this is capable even of loving his enemies, of forgiving and understanding those who persecute him. The New Situation permits him to live beyond himself and his own feelings; it heals him because he knows that he is a beloved child of the Father, called to be with Him and configure himself to Him.
>
> Conversion also reaches into someone's pocket, reaching not only who he is but what he possesses; not to be seen by others but solely to bring glory to God. He discovers the pleasure and the power of prayer, calls God "Father," learns to be self-sacrificing and to fast; he encounters the meaning of sacrifice. *The face of the person who lives in the New Situation is more luminous. Even his look and his facial features are transformed.*

All of this is inspired by the Sermon on the Mount. The writer goes on to say:

> He trusts in providence and the power of prayer, having experienced this power for himself; he is capable of liberating himself from old vices and habits that hinder him from living his faith well; he knows how to enter through the narrow gate; and he abandons idols and false prophets. He has deeper knowledge of the faith, is more capable of recognizing what

is true and good by its fruits, meditates on the Word, begins to live a life based on Gospel values, turns to God through his works, and performs works of mercy. He never ceases to be amazed by the teachings of Jesus; he follows Christ as his near and authoritative Master.

This all produces a certain harmony, a Christian lifestyle well summarized above and deserving of celebration.

The Sermon on the Mount has extraordinary power. Whoever decides to live these three chapters, Matthew 5–7, will find there all he needs to follow the teachings of Christ and embody the Christian way of life.

### Saints and Radicals

I will return again to the question that is at the root of doubts about the Sermon on the Mount: is it really possible to live this teaching, or is it a utopia—something toward which we are moving but will never reach?

The Church and the saints teach us that it is possible to live the Beatitudes. Jesus himself lived them radically and so did the saints. *The saints not only lived these Beatitudes but applied them in very different contexts. If Mother Teresa of Calcutta lived the Sermon on the Mount, then, yes, we can too.*

In our home diocese of Cruz del Eje, Argentina, we have the example of St. José Gabriel del Rosario Brochero: "Saint Cura Brochero."[4] The distinctive features of his life are very

---

[4]     In the sanctuary of "Our Lady of Transit," in Villa Cura Brochero, Argentina, I had the grace of receiving my priestly ordination, as have many of the priests of the Saint John Society; in the place where Brochero's remains are.

well presented in the prayer we all prayed to ask for his canonization: "*Lord, from whom comes every perfect gift, you . . . illuminated* [St. Cura Brochero] for his missionary zeal, his evangelical preaching, and his poor and self-sacrificing life." This prayer emphasizes his ardent desire to reach those who were furthest away through his preaching, which—like Christ's—was deep, simple, and adapted to his listeners,[5] and his life, which was made a total offering for the whole flock that was entrusted to him. His evangelical life was a living reflection of the life of Jesus, totally inspired by the Sermon on the Mount in the context of western Córdoba from the end of the nineteenth century to the beginning of the twentieth century. That is how the saints are. And that is why today there are still such abundant fruits, both human and Christian, from the life of Cura Brochero.

In a letter to another priest, Brochero describes how his helpers should be, if any should be sent to him: he wants them detached, poor, attentive to spiritual life, zealous for the flock, gentle with the people, and even more gentle with

---

5    "I am going to preach two missions, one which begins tomorrow in the Ingenio Santa Ana. But what I want to tell you is the text with which I broke through in [inviting the people to] the first mission: this was a black cow, that all of my listeners could see. I said that, just as that cow was a sign and an indicator of the Engineer called the Trinity, in the same way all of us Christians are also signed and marked by God; but that God didn't brand us in our leg, or our stomach, or our ribs, but rather in our soul, and that God didn't give us a sign on our ears, but rather on our foreheads because the sign of God is the holy cross, and his branding mark is the faith, and he puts this in our soul." Letter from St. Cura Brochero to Guillermo Molina, 1901. El Cura Brochero: Cartas y Sermlones. Buenos Aires: La Oficina del Libro de la Conferencia Episcopal de Argentina. Translation is mine.

the poorest. You can clearly see the echo, the harmony, between the text of his letter and chapters five through seven of Matthew's Gospel:

> The Priest will make sure that his belongings are also those of his helpers; that is, he will see to not reserve anything from them. . . . The helpers will tell Cura Brochero anything they see wrong with his behavior toward them or with his faithful or any particular persons, in order that he may amend the said wrong and explain to them his reason for acting so. . . . The helpers need to make a day of retreat each month together with the Cura and need to go to confession once a week unless distance or another circumstance impede this frequency; but they will go as soon as possible, with luck not any longer than every 15 or 20 days. The Cura will set the example for them, confessing first with one and then with another. . . . Inasmuch as the faithful are greater sinners or more rough or uncivilized, they should be treated with more sweetness and kindness in the confessional, in the pulpit and even in familiar interactions. And if something is found that is worthy of challenge, they will advise the Cura so that he can make the correction. Then the faithful won't feel resentment toward the helpers, but rather with the Cura, because he already knows how to correct them. . . . They will perform burials and functions . . . at least without the tariff, because that way they will gain . . . the reputation of being detached. . . . They will help the Cura to confess the healthy left and right; and they can preach each time that they want to and are able to, because they will always have listeners.[6]

Because the SSJ was born in his diocese and grew under his mantle, we want the SSJ to take him as intercessor and model, above all in those features of his prayer that have been listed.[7]

---

[6]    Letter to Father Filemón Cabañillas, 1884.

[7]    On the first page of our constitutions, we read, *"It is the Church that evangelizes through our apostolate. She herself is a Gospel. In effect,*

All of the saints—each one in his or her way and in very different situations—lived the Beatitudes inspired by Jesus and moved by the Holy Spirit. As C. S. Lewis says, the saints are all very different, not all the same.[8] The world is repetitive, and sinners too are all the same.

When those of you who are studying to become priests are ordained, you will see this when you receive the people who come to confession with you. People say, "No, Father, for you to confess me you'll need to set aside three days!" And one thinks, and even says to them, "Um, okay, come, you're not going to surprise me!" I wish someone would surprise me, but no. All the sins of us humans are very similar. After original sin, we are not very original in our sins; all of them are rather predictable.

In contrast, virtues are all different. In the measure in which we grow in virtue, people come to differentiate themselves from one another. We Christians also go through this process, and our challenge—the challenge that Christ calls us to personally—is to always do it in conformity with this Sermon, with his teachings.

Scripture says, for example, "Let love be sincere; hate what is evil, hold on to what is good: love one another with

---

*evangelizing is an ecclesial act and represents the faith of the universal Church. It means that we announce Christ with the faith of Mary, with the faith of Peter and Paul, of Athanasius and of Jerome, of Augustine and of Francis of Assisi, of Teresa of Jesus, of Toribius of Mogrovejo, of Philip Neri, of Cardinal Newman, of Cura Brochero and of the whole People of God. God wants to give the gift of faith through the mediation of the Church in each one of us."*

[8]   "How monotonously alike all the great tyrants and conquerors have been: how gloriously different are the saints." C. S. Lewis, *Mere Christianity*. San Francisco: HarperOne, 2000. p. 226.

mutual affection; anticipate one another in showing honor. Do not grow slack in zeal, be fervent in prayer, serve the Lord. Rejoice in hope, endure in affliction, persevere in prayer. Contribute to the needs of the holy ones, exercise hospitality. Bless those who persecute you . . ."[9] and it goes on. It is the Sermon on the Mount in a different key.

The Sermon on the Mount is to be lived, and you can indeed live it, in the measure in which you have received it. And you received it so that you can begin to live it.

## The Beatitudes and the Kingdom

When I asked for "homework" before the retreat, Fr. Rodrigo sent this reflection to me: *"None of the Beatitudes are possible if there is not first the Kingdom. The Kingdom is first; the Beatitudes are the consequence of the Kingdom. And perhaps through them we come to comprehend what the Kingdom is. The Kingdom is the life of God received in us, mediated through our interior."*

The Beatitudes are not possible if there is not first the kingdom within us. We receive the kingdom, and that is why we can live them.

I propose that you ask to "fall in love" with this lifestyle—to fall in love in the sense of seeing that it is possible for you to live like this, and that you are called to this life: not fifteen years from now, but today.

We have to adopt this lifestyle with a certain radicality— not with absolute perfection, but definitely with the force of what seems to us primordial; it is essential and of the first

---

[9]    Rom 12:9ff.

priority. Yes, we are already living this to a certain extent. But we are called to more: to live the Beatitudes—the teachings of Christ—with deep love.

Ask to fall in love with them and see their beauty, *to be evangelical men with the zest of the Gospel.* We need communities for the New Evangelization that radiate Christ with the zeal of the Gospel.

The preaching of Jesus—particularly at the beginning—hinges upon the proclamation of the coming kingdom, *which is deeply connected with the proclamation and experience of the paternity of God.*

The New Situation is given through our new relationship with God as Father, in Christ Jesus. The relationship of Jesus with his Father can be understood in light of the proclamation of the kingdom and vice versa: the proclamation of the kingdom is understood in the relationship of Jesus with his Father.

It's as if Christ were to say, "The kingdom is being my Father's child: come, and participate in this relationship. *When you are children of my Father—through the gift which I am going to give you—you will understand what it is to live by providence, to know how to forgive, and to have a unified love, because that is the kingdom of my Father. Come and enter into that new relationship to which you are called, you who are blessed by my Father!"*

Entering into the New Situation is entering into the sonship of Jesus—a relationship that is healthy, healing, and deeply rooted in the heart. And that is why, at the heart of the Sermon on the Mount, we find the prayer of the Our Father. "This is how you are to pray . . ." And Jesus speaks the Our Father.

## Exercise

We hold that the good news of the kingdom, proclaimed by Jesus, is the message that in him there is a New Situation. I propose two exercises for you:

1. Let's start first with the whole, and later look at the parts. Does this message call to me? Can I see that this is a message that's relevant to the here and now?

   Do I feel that this message is becoming incarnate in me and that I am soaking in what I proclaim? Is it becoming a reality in me? How?

   Let's return now to the Sermon on the Mount, which is the New Situation developed. What aspects of these teachings do I feel I am able to better bring to life?

   As we have already said, *the Sermon on the Mount is the Christian lifestyle: the development of the New Situation in its different relationships.*

   Have we experienced life in Christ? We should be messengers of a single message; that is why Jesus has called us to form part of this society. What is your message? What message do you announce with your life, your words, and your attitude?

   Of course, no one perfectly incarnates the Sermon on the Mount; we all incarnate some aspects more than others. But we can always come back to contemplate Jesus in his public life announcing the Good News of the kingdom: for example, Matthew 4:23 and Matthew 9:35. And we can ask again with great trust: *Give me your word, your mission; give it to me and to all of us. We want to form a community of the saved, capable of transmitting our sentiments and experiences.*

2.  Next, I propose that you contemplate Christ preaching the kingdom. In the Gospel of Matthew 4:23, it says, "He went around all of Galilee, teaching in their synagogues, proclaiming the gospel of the kingdom, and curing every disease and illness among the people."

You will notice that the Sermon on the Mount begins right after this in chapter 5, stretching through chapter 7. Chapter 8 then describes the signs that corroborate and ratify this teaching. Jesus doesn't just teach; with his healings, he manifests that the kingdom of God described in the Sermon on the Mount is already at work, already present in him. It's a matter of both words and works. This section extends until the end of chapter 9, which culminates with the same phrase, in verse 35, "Jesus went around to all the towns and villages, teaching in their synagogues, proclaiming the gospel of the kingdom, and curing every disease and illness."

That is called *inclusion* in the Bible: when the same text is repeated at the beginning and the end of a passage as if it were quotation marks. Its purpose is to show that everything included in that text is one great unity. The Sermon on the Mount and its signs open and close with this inclusion: the image of Jesus preaching in his public life. These texts are on the first page of our constitutions. In his public life, Jesus preaches the kingdom described in Matthew 5–7 and puts its signs described in Matthew 8–9 into effect.

So contemplate the image of Jesus preaching and living the kingdom. Ask that you, and all of us, may be like him—may be able to live the public life of Jesus, preaching the message of new life laid out in the Sermon on the Mount.

# CONCLUSION: BLESSED ARE THOSE WHO HAVE NOT SEEN AND HAVE BELIEVED

## The Gospel Is Filled With and Penetrated by the Beatitudes

THERE are other Beatitudes in the Gospel. For example, in Luke, Jesus says that the eyes of the disciples are already blessed to see what they are seeing,[1] because many would have liked to see but did not.

*Peter, after his confession at Caesarea,* is told, "Blessed are you, Simon, son of Jonah. For flesh and blood has not revealed this to you, but my heavenly Father."[2] Jesus also says, "Blessed is the one who takes no offence at me,"[3] and "Blessed are those who have not seen and have believed."[4]

Mary, the Mother of Jesus, is especially blessed for having believed. "Blessed are you who believed that what was spoken to you by the Lord would be fulfilled,"[5] Elizabeth says to Mary. On another occasion, Jesus responds to the woman who praised his mother for birthing and raising

---

[1]    Lk 10:23.
[2]    Mt 16:17.
[3]    Mt 11:6.
[4]    Jn 20:29.
[5]    Lk 1:45.

him, "Blessed are those who hear the word of God and observe it."[6]

As you can see, the Beatitudes are not exclusive to the Sermon on the Mount. Not only the Gospel, but other books of the New Testament are filled with Beatitudes. For example, Jesus proclaims *blessed* those who witnessed his works and words: "Blessed are your eyes, because they see, and your ears, because they hear."[7] And in the Acts of the Apostles, Luke transmits a Beatitude of Jesus that is not registered in any of the Gospels: "It is more blessed to give than to receive."[8]

I would like to conclude these meditations with one of these other Beatitudes, proclaimed by Jesus to the astonishment of the incredulous Thomas: "*Blessed are those who have not seen and have believed.*"[9]

Being able to believe, and to accept with trust and love a Presence that manifests himself in our life, is a grace—an unmerited gift. Effectively, faith is possible because there is a revelation of the one who is the object of our faith, and we are given an encounter with him. Thus, in the beginning of the spiritual life, believing is as easy and simple as accepting a piece of evidence: that of the one who is present and revealed by the power of love, circumstances, interactions with others, and the signs of Providence. It is not visible or palpable evidence, but something like an interior anointing that makes it easy to open the heart and say, *I believe!*

It is the moment of the "first conversion," when the

---

6      Lk 11:28.
7      Mt 13:16.
8      Acts 20:35.
9      Jn 20:29.

person appropriates the faith that he perhaps had received with his education or through cultural possession, and recognizes himself as a believer with the authenticity of a deeply free and personal act. From then on, everything becomes simple, because believing in this way goes hand in hand with growth. The changes, steps, and attitudes of Christian life begin to develop.

It is an astonishing response to an unexpected revelation. God gives faith as a grace when he makes himself present. He gives the light and the object of the light; or, rather, the Object brings its own light in order to be seen. One of the missionaries wrote, "If he had not introduced himself, I would not have been capable of a transforming act of faith. Because he came, I saw."

Faith is a response to a Presence! Just as the eye sees the light, faith is the organ through which we see Christ. And just as the eye begins to function when there is light, so faith begins to function when the Object, Christ, reveals himself. We can distinguish, but not separate, these two things: Christ making himself present in our life, and faith receiving him. In this sense, faith is the light of Christ that shines over us. We have the capacity to perceive the light of Christ and, when he appears, to capture his beauty, because the human heart is made for him. But that perception can also be denied. We can close our eyes and remain in darkness out of fear, or because we don't want to change due to selfishness or distrust. This is the nucleus of faith: to see him because he has made himself present, and to believe and trust because I saw him. Therefore, blessed are you if you have faith!

Faith is grace. It is the highest grade of reason—reason's

most worthy act—because through the very act of believing, reason recognizes its limits; it cannot give itself faith. Reason can weave together all the reasons for convenience, but it cannot propel itself to believe. To go from plausibility to certainty requires the grace of first being encountered by him. St. Paul testifies to this in his letter to the Philippians: "I continue my pursuit in the hope that I may possess it, *since I have indeed been taken possession of by Christ Jesus.*"[10]

This helps us understand the faith of many poor people. It is not an immature or barely "enlightened" faith, even though it still can and should be formed. It is an authentic faith, because God has visited them with his predilection. So Mary sings in her thanksgiving: "He has looked upon his handmaid's lowliness."[11] They frequently "see" things with more clarity, even though they cannot give the philosophical reasons for it. They do not have so many qualms in accepting that which has been given to them gratuitously.

I invite you also to give thanks for God's gratuity in revealing himself to you. Having read this book supposes a desire to live the Beatitudes, which are the "lifestyle of Jesus." Having that desire supposes faith; and in order to be able to believe, it is necessary that he be made present.

So, from the first of the Beatitudes all the way up to the end of John's Gospel, there is a common thread. It is those who are poor in spirit who find themselves more prepared to believe, but it is also true that, in believing, even the more self-sufficient of us become more and more poor—more and more receptive to the gift of God. Faith brings us, little

---

[10]    Phil 3:12.
[11]    Lk 1:48.

by little, to humility, and purifies us. In comprehension, man may still dominate, but through belief, he is brought to trust. That is why God wants faith—why it is a virtue that we greatly need. Faith prepares us for an even greater gift: the gift of the definitive encounter.

Blessed are you if you are satisfied with the received evidence—if you can say to Jesus that you don't need more light, that what you have received from him is enough for trust, love, and giving of yourself.

# CONCLUDING MEDITATION: LIVING THE SERMON ON THE MOUNT AUTHENTICALLY[1]

## The Authenticity of Christ

IN this meditation, let us contemplate the authenticity of Christ, *his human authenticity: everything in him reflects what he is.*

Reading the answers you sent me about the Beatitude of the pure of heart, it caught my attention that while many people have recognized the link between purity and chastity, you went beyond chastity to relate purity to a certain cleanness and transparency of life. Someone with a clean heart is authentic and whole: someone who is what he is before God and men, and who relates with others through that.

So it is with Jesus Christ. Everything in him reflects the Son of the Father, who comes to inaugurate the kingdom; that is his deepest identity and what is seen in his life. He reflects and incarnates it, acts on it, promotes, teaches, and realizes it on the cross and in his resurrection, and offers it through the Holy Spirit; he communicates the grace of his Spirit.

He is a person who is centered and not dispersed—a

---

[1]  Although this mediation was originally addressed to the members of the Saint John Society, it can be adapted to your own situation and used for personal reflection.

person who knows how to rest and love, and who does
it within the framework of a profound unity of life. We
see this, for example, in the Gospel of John, where Jesus
says, "My food is to do the will of the one who sent me
and to complete his work."² Do you remember when Jesus
was with the Samaritan, and the apostles, hearing him say
this, asked themselves, "Could someone have brought him
something to eat?" Of course Jesus ate, but in his way of life
and in his message, his foundation of nourishment—his
energy, what made him alive and moved him each day—
was "to do the will of the one who sent me." Later Jesus says,
"My Father is at work until now, so I am at work."³

Christ has a vision; he knows where he is going, and he
has discernment. He is establishing that kingdom that he
came to inaugurate in his own person, step by step. He has
a project, a plan of action that he elaborated in dialogue
with his Father, illuminated by the interior lights of the
Spirit.

That is why we see him announcing the kingdom at
the beginning of his public life—a concept that everyone
could understand—and performing many miracles. After
the confession of Peter at Caesarea Philippi, there are fewer
miracles. Jesus begins to announce the cross. Finally, when
it is the moment to go to Jerusalem, he sets his face.⁴ There
is a progression.

He even teaches this discernment to his apostles: *The
fields are ready; lift up your eyes, look.*⁵ In other words, pay

²    Jn 4:34.
³    Jn 5:17.
⁴    Lk 9:51.
⁵    See Jn 5:34.

attention to what is happening. And he feels an ardent love for what he has to do—for his Father and his own, for those who accompany him. He says, "I have eagerly desired to eat this Passover with you,"[6] and to be with you.

He has a mission to complete and he carries it out right on schedule, with a great fidelity and authenticity. He incarnates the radicality that he preaches. He is what he is. I think that this trait of authenticity in the humanity of Christ is very important, because we are also called to grow in authenticity.

*Though we are not Christ, we appropriate him little by little through the vocation we have received*—the vocation to Christian life, through the call at Baptism and through consecrated life. The public life of Jesus is the model for our lives. Step by step we reach that maturity—that stature in Christ—and feel more and more authentic in who we are. The distance between the "real me" and the "ideal me" grows smaller, and in that way, we become more authentic.

You are being formed to be priests. Some of you are philosophy students, some have finished philosophy and are preparing to study theology, and some are still beginning but are in a stage of integral formation: human, intellectual, community, spiritual, and apostolic. Formation is the time for "docibilitas," as Fr. Cencini puts it[7]—the time during which you let yourself be filled more powerfully by the humanity of Christ.

That is why you study, live in community, and do what you do. The power of each stage of formation—at least of

---

6    Lk 22:15.
7    See Amedeo Cencini, *Por amor, con amor, en el amor.* Ed. Sígueme, 2007.

the initial formation—is *becoming more authentically who you are called to be.*

### Exercise

Now, I propose that you ask the Lord for the grace to be more authentic:

> "Lord, give me the grace to configure my life to yours right now, today; let my spiritual life be a life in Christ; let my way of life be your public life.
>
> "Let the purpose of my life be to live as a missionary working with students, professionals and the poorest.
>
> "Let this be authentic in me! Let me be able to embrace this mission as a deeply personal identity. You have called me from my mother's womb to live this. I beg you, Jesus, let my personal message be the New Situation; let my lifestyle irradiate the Sermon on the Mount; let me be the best possible me that I can be, by your grace."

Some time ago, I was speaking with a monk whom I met in the United States, and he told me that one day he and his companions were engaged in small talk at the dinner table. So he said, "Brothers, we're monks. Let's drop this empty talk and speak of Christ. Enough with empty talking! What are we even talking about? Let's speak like monks if we're monks." He told me of this casually in passing, but he was right. I like what he said very much; monks should speak like monks, and among themselves they should speak about the concerns of monks. And we should speak and live like missionaries of the New Evangelization, irradiating Christ at all times: seven days a week, twenty-four hours a day.

That is authenticity: being what we are, everywhere we go. Of course, we are sinners and sin is interior division, so we don't always have that authenticity; but how beautiful it is to long for that authenticity.

*Oh, Lord! If only I could be more authentic! If only I could better incarnate all of this more and more! I am going to pray—not because "I have to" pray, but because I desire it from my deepest identity. I am going to the slums, not because I have to go to the slums on Saturday, but because of much more than that. I am studying all day; please, Lord, let me at least go once a week to the poorest and speak with them. Please don't take that from me.* And the prayer goes on.

We want our authenticity to come from the impulse of the New Situation in Christ, from an identity deeply anchored in Christ. Even so, we have to ask him more for it; because for the one who lives in Christ, the law is not necessary. During formation there should be no need for superiors, rules, or monitors; realistically, they are needed, because we need someone to guide us—but you understand what I'm trying to say. It would be marvelous if it could be that way. *Our rule is there, the constitutions are there, because they protect and orient an identity, but the one who lives in Christ overcomes this and goes beyond it.*

The other day, one of the priests in Córdoba, Fr. Máximo—who goes to activities like the Cenacle, where 350 high school students participate, and who helps in the very large adult Fragua group—said to me, "A ton of people already come here. But I want to leave and go farther out; I don't want to care only for "these many who come" already on their own, because calling others is part of our life. I do not want to lose contact with the ones who do not believe." And I like that—that is authenticity.

An authentic identity thinks: *This is well and good, but I am a missionary. I want some opportunities to leave here and be in contact with the frontiers of faith, because that is what I am: a missionary.*

Authenticity is important because circumstances change, and if we are not authentic, we begin to change who we are with them. We begin to accommodate ourselves to those changing circumstances. However, if there we are authentic in who we are, well, we will be able to act authentically wherever we may be, because who we are is already in us.

*Glory be to the Father, and to the Son, and to the Holy Spirit. As it was in the beginning, is now, and will be forever. Amen.*

# APPENDIX: AN EXAMINATION OF CONSCIENCE BASED ON THE BEATITUDES

THE best way of taking the evangelical Beatitudes we have meditated upon seriously is to use them as a mirror for a truly "evangelical" examination of conscience. James says all of Scripture is like a mirror in which the believer should look at himself calmly and without hurry in order to know himself truly "as he is,"[1] and the Beatitudes are the best way of doing so.

*"Blessed are the poor in spirit, for theirs is the kingdom of God."* Am I poor in spirit, poor from within, abandoned to God in everything? Am I free and detached from earthly goods? What does money mean to me? Do I try to live a sober and simple lifestyle—that of a consecrated person who wants to bear witness to the Gospel? Does the poverty of the poor cause me pain? Am I in solidarity with them? Am I faithful to cleaning, maintenance, and material labor? Do I complain when I lack something necessary, or do I face it with a supernatural spirit? Do I love poverty inasmuch as it configures me to the poor Christ?

*"Blessed are they who mourn, for they will be comforted."* Do I think of affliction as a disgrace and a punishment, as do those in the world; or do I see it as an opportunity to configure myself to Christ? What causes my sadness:

---

[1]  See Jas 1:23–25.

the motives of God or those of the world? Do I seek to
console others, or only to be consoled myself? What are my
apostolic sufferings? Do I know how to keep the difficult
things that happen to me a secret between me and God,
without telling everyone? How is my joy? How do I testify
to it? What feeds it? How is my supernatural hope? Does it
have any practical relevance for me?

"*Blessed are the meek (patient), for they will inherit the
land.*" Am I meek? Is there violence in my actions, even if
it be in words or thoughts? Do I conquer anger outside and
inside of me? Am I gentle and affable with my neighbors?
Do I have patience for suffering? Do I know how to wait?

"*Blessed are they who hunger and thirst for righteousness,
for they will be satisfied.*" Do I hunger and thirst for holiness? Do I tend toward holiness, or have I resigned myself,
perhaps for some time, to mediocrity and lukewarmness?
Do I hunger and thirst for myself and others to live in the
New Situation and bring about Christ's kingdom? Is this
hunger reflected in my apostolic zeal, or am I satisfied?

"*Blessed are the merciful, for they will be shown mercy.*"
Am I merciful? Before the error of a brother or coworker,
do I react with judgment or with mercy? Jesus felt compassion for people: do I? Have I been the forgiven servant who
didn't know how to forgive his fellow servant? How many
times have I casually asked for and received the mercy of
God for my sins without realizing the price Christ paid to
give it to me? Do I foster rash judgments? Do I practice
hospitality? Do I willingly offer my service? Is it pleasant to
live with me?

"*Blessed are the clean of heart, for they will see God.*" Am
I pure of heart? Pure in my intentions? When I say "yes,"

is it yes, and when I say "no," is it no, like Jesus? There is a purity of heart, purity of lips, purity of eyes, purity of the body ... Do I seek to cultivate these very necessary purities?

"*Blessed are the peacemakers, for they will be called children of God.*" Do I work for peace? Do I make peace between differing parties? How do I behave when there is a conflict of opinion or interests? Do I make the effort to speak always and only of the good, with positive words, and do I let all that is bad—like gossip and what could sow discord—fall away to nothing? Is the peace of God in my heart? If not, then why?

"*Blessed are they who are persecuted for the sake of righteousness, for theirs is the kingdom of heaven.*" Am I ready to suffer in silence for the Gospel? How do I react before any injustice or offense that I receive? Am I humble, with a sense of reparation?